SMASHING
THE GRASS CEILING

A Women's Guide to
Mastering Golf for
Business Success

FAREEN SAMJI
MICHELLE HARRIS

ISBN: 978-0-9959318-0-0 (sc)
ISBN: 978-0-9959318-1-7 (e)

Library of Congress Control Number: 2017906579

Cover Photo Credit: Robyn S Russell Photography
Photography on location at Dundas Valley Golf & Curling Club

Lulu Publishing Services rev. date: 2/5/2018

Writing this book was one of the hardest things I have done. It would not have been possible to do without the help of a team of amazing, efficient and strong women. From the women who lent me their ear to the women who took the time to provide their feedback - thank you. To Ann and the kids, thank you for bearing with me through the evenings and the weekends.

A special thank you to:

Michele Bailey
Thie Convery
Melanie Cunnigham
Lowie Crisp
Jasmina Garbus
Leila Hurley
Helen Knowles (aka the interpreter)
Rosanne Longo
Dr. Pamela Ritchie
Mercer Smith
Jennifer Walker

To the women who allowed me share their stories - thank you:

Marlane Robertson
Caroline Johnson
Michelle Cederberg
Emily Phillips Teh
Mary Dilly
Joan Davis
Shannon Bowen-Smed
Amy Kasianiuk
Michelle Harris
Maggie Loefler

The amazing women at 127 Strategies: for pushing me to be better

Ann Loree: For supporting me so that I could play professional golf. For enabling me to do everything I want to do

Michelle Harris: My partner in words. Thank you for sharing your big beautiful brain with me. It has only just begun

FOREWORD

I am absolutely honoured to write the foreword for Fareen's new Book *"Smashing The Grass Ceiling."* Fareen has been smashing that ceiling her whole life! She never sees limits, only possibilities and goals. She is inspiring, motivational and passionate about everything she sets out to do. Fareen's message is one that needs to be shared and heard. I have the good fortune of working with women in golf around North America both in a corporate and recreational capacity. I participate in over 25 events each year and 75-80% of the participants are men. The women are back in the office doing the work while the guys are doing the networking. *"Smashing The Grass Ceiling"* gives women the tools they need to understand this great game of golf, to get the courage to pick up the sticks for the first time or even if it has been a long time, and to reap the rewards of playing golf both for personal, wellness and corporate gains. Fareen will help you feel comfortable and confident to smash your own grass ceiling!

Lisa "Longball" Vlooswyk

7-Time Canadian Long Drive Champion
Keynote Speaker
Golf/Travel Journalist
Golf Entertainer

CONTENTS

THE GRASS CEILING

Steph, a good friend of mine, asked me to be the fourth golfer in a charity golf tournament. She had invited two of her male clients and wanted to balance out the foursome with two ladies. I was excited for the opportunity to get out of the office and spend some time outside. When we got to the event I looked around and noticed that over 90% of golfers there were men. This is typical of most golf events I go to. It has always bothered me that more women don't use golf as a business building tool because men have been using it to advance their career interests for years.

Something interesting happens when people are on the golf course, outside, surrounded by other people who are happy to be out of the office as well, they relax! It's a casual non-threatening networking atmosphere. Sure you can bring a client to a restaurant but it's not all that different from an office or board room environment. Take that same person to a beautiful park like setting with the shared goal of playing a game and you quickly find common ground, laugh and make memories together.

The term "relationship building" is thrown around all the time, but what it means to me is turning strangers into friends. Playing golf with someone allows you the opportunity to take a business connection and deepen that relationship. You get the chance to spend a few hours of uninterrupted time with someone, without their electronic devices or yours. It allows you to become emotionally invested in each other's lives by sharing stories and experiences, unlike the types of interactions you would typically have standing around at a networking event. Imagine playing with a potential client and having two hours of uninterrupted time to show them that you are respectful, generous, empathetic, trustworthy, confident and humble. To actually have them get to know the real *you* a little better. When you can create that kind of intimate relationship with someone, you care about their goals and they care about yours. You will stand out in their mind. They will want to buy from you, fundraise for your cause or put your name forward for a promotion because you are now more than just business associates. You can show off your leadership skills, your ability to deal with frustration and your character. A business lunch or networking event can't give you that incredible opportunity.

I asked Steph how long she had been using golf as a business tool, and she told me that she hadn't always used golf for business, in fact, she never even thought about it till her last job in a big bank. When she got hired, she was told she needed to learn the game and was even given a set of golf clubs by her boss, but after trying it a couple of times, she put it off. What she did notice was that during the week several of her colleagues, including her boss would go out golfing with clients or get invited to golf in community events, and she was left behind in the office. She was worried that her game was not good enough to join them and that she didn't have the time to get better with her work and family commitments. Many of the women that I have coached over the years are not willing to be vulnerable in front of clients or coworkers, so they hold off using golf until they can improve their game. I find this curious because most men I know are fearless about playing bad golf! Watch them golfing out there, they are not that good! They understand that it's the setting that is important, not their skill level.

Once Steph left the bank and started her own company, she began to focus on golfing as a key customer retention and acquisition strategy. She is an absolute rock star in her world, mom of three kids, climbed through the ranks in her previous job and is now doing her own thing and killing it. Even though she is still a beginner golfer, the event she invited me to was for a youth charity she believed in and it was an excellent opportunity to spend some time with her clients. Steph had finally figured it out. *You don't need to be a good golfer to be able to use golf to build relationships, entertain clients, spend time with friends and family, or raise money for charity.* What you do need to know is golf etiquette, how to keep up, how to manage your emotions and how to have fun on the golf course. You can be a pro golfer out there, but it doesn't mean that you will be a person that others want to be around on the golf course. People remember people they like. People do business with people they like.

I wrote this book because there are thousands of books and videos that can teach you how to swing a club or make a putt, but what most coaches miss are the social and emotional interactions around the game. Steph confided that before she made golf a priority, she had taken a few lessons and played a round or two with her husband but found it too difficult and lost interest. I have heard variations of this story so many times from many different women: the game is hard, there are all these rules, no one will want to play with us anyway, it's too stressful when there is a group behind pushing us. I get it. There are barriers that keep professional women from taking advantage of what the game has to offer.

I cannot tell you the number of times I have shown up to the first tee paired with men and they roll their eyes at their misfortune of being paired with a woman. Their automatic assumption is that we will ruin their day out on the course. Golf can be perceived as having complicated rules and etiquette which can be intimidating for some - but it doesn't need to be! I have always seen this as a kind of 'grass ceiling' that we need to smash! The purpose of this book is to inspire women to get out on the golf course and to teach you how to use golf to create meaningful business connections. This book is your resource guide to feeling confident and knowing how to handle yourself on the golf course so that you can join or invite anyone for a round with you.

What you will learn from this book

Smashing The Grass Ceiling will share with you the knowledge you *actually* need to play the game and the strategies you need to make you invincible out on the course. By the end of the book you will:

- confidently know your way around a golf course and how to play the game

- learn the etiquette of how to behave on the golf course

- know which rules of golf are important to follow

- recognize the various golf personalities you'll see on the course so that you can manage them and prevent yourself from becoming one of them

- master strategies to manage your own emotions

- learn how to participate in charity golf tournaments

- learn how to use golf as a social and business networking tool

If you are really new to the game and need help with how to take lessons and get the right equipment, this book can still help! The first few chapters will cover this in detail and in the appendix you will find a summary on what equipment you need and what each club is supposed to do. If you have already taken lessons and have the equipment you need, skip those chapters and read on.

My story

I am a business owner, wife, mother, mentor, athlete, teacher and volunteer. I run a family business with my two brothers and we own orthotic and orthopedic shoe clinics as well as a manufacturing facility. I am very active in my community, am integral to a few major community fundraisers and sit on several committees and boards. Golf has been instrumental in my success because it has given me the opportunity to spend time with my family and build relationships with key business influencers. Getting involved in golf events as a participant and as a sponsor has helped me position our business as an active supporter of our community and aligns us with causes that make a difference in people's lives. I use golf as a way to get face time with vendors, suppliers, employees and clients.

When you put people in a situation where they have to manage potential embarrassment, to practice humility, engage in decision making, show respect, and act honestly amongst their peers who are watching their every move, you will quickly find the people you want to do business with! When you show people that you can do those things well, they will have respect for you and will want to do business with you. I have seen professional adults act like children throwing tantrums, get moody when things don't go their way on the golf course, and who are clearly unable to deal with frustration. Observe the interactions some golfers have with the beverage cart server and you'll figure out quickly if you want to do business with them!

I started playing young

I started playing golf when I was ten years old in Mombasa, Kenya. When I tell people that I am from Kenya, they look at me with a puzzled look because I look like I'm from India. Yes, I have Indian heritage, but I am fourth generation Kenyan and since Kenya and India were both colonized by the British, you will find Indians not only in Kenya but throughout East Africa.

As I look at those same folks trying to internalize how I can be African but look Indian, I see the next thought cross their face – did she say she started playing golf in Kenya? Maybe they had images of lions and elephants roaming around, but Kenya has a very rich golfing history because our colonizers liked to play golf.

My journey actually began with my mum. When I was ten, my mum Shaida finally took advantage of the family membership to the Mombasa Golf Club that my dad Abdul bought years before they had kids. Mum started talking about how much she liked golf around the dinner table and tried to encourage us kids to take up the game. We wanted nothing to do with it. Golf was not a game that the cool kids played. In true parental fashion, she bribed me to get me to go to the driving range to try it out. I realized pretty quickly that if I played golf, I would get her all to myself and wouldn't have to share her with my brothers.

The senior members of the club were quite intrigued that a kid was interested in the game and when they saw me out on the range, they came down and gave me a few pointers. I also took some lessons from the resident pro, watched all the good golfers and tried to emulate their swings. Around this time, Dad went on a business trip to London and brought me back a *How to Play Golf* video that Mum and I watched several times and then practised what we had learned out on the course. There wasn't organized junior golf in Kenya at the time so all the events I played in were with and against adults. I progressed quickly and within a couple of years I was winning local and regional golf events.

My weekends were spent competing in club tournaments and in any given event I might be drawn to play with my school principal, my dentist, my doctor, my dad's lawyer, insurance broker or banker - professional people established in their careers. What amazed me as a kid surrounded by adults was the way in which their personalities changed on the golf course. When good shots were being hit, everyone was all smiles, but when bad shots were hit, the smiles were replaced with pouts, excuses and tantrums. And amazingly some of these educated people lost the ability to count past eight!

I spent hours observing adults networking on the golf course and I learned pretty quickly not only the rules and etiquette of the game but also how to handle myself around people much older than me. I credit golf with teaching me the social skills that have served me well in my current entrepreneurial journey.

Pro golf was my hardest job

I came to Canada for a university education sponsored by my uncle who was an egg farmer in Ontario. Working on the egg farm helped reinforce the value of hard work and discipline. I needed those values when I decided to try my hand at professional golf after graduating. I started as a club pro at Mill Run, in Uxbridge, Ontario. I got my CPGA credentials, started teaching lessons and then went on tour full-time to play golf on the mini tours all over the world. I joined the LPGA teaching division for a few years and taught golf lessons in the off-season to earn enough money to go out on tour for another season. Sounds glamorous doesn't it? Travelling the world playing golf? Actually, it was horrible. Playing professionally was a total grind and by far the hardest thing I have ever done.

Week after week, I put myself and my game on display in front of strangers. Whether you're a pro playing against your peers or in a ladies league playing with your best friend, everyone gets nervous teeing off. More times than I want to admit, I'd stand over the tee, heart pounding, hands shaking waiting to take my first swing of the day after being announced to the crowd. With my driver in hand, I would take that first swing and inevitably, my ball would end up in the trees on the left and I would be two penalty strokes in the hole. The silence and discomfort from the crowd was palpable. Did that shot define my character? I'm supposed to be a pro and yet I hit it out of bounds - I must be a fraud, right? As I write these words I realize how ludicrous it sounds. Trust me, golf is not rational. There are not many situations in life where we can fail so publicly at something. Golf can make you question your confidence, your self-esteem and your desire to keep playing the game.

However, when you strike a driver in the sweet spot of the club face and you see that little ball sail straight down the middle of the fairway or when you make a long putt and watch the ball drop into the hole, it's a total high. It feels like the easiest game in the world. In an entire round of golf, you may only have one moment like that but it's enough to keep you coming back for more. Golf is a fun game to play and *having fun with the people you want to do business with is a great way to build significant, lasting relationships*.

Reigniting my passion for golf with long drive

I left the world of professional golf after four years to start my career and my family and worked diligently to build my business. Trying to balance family life, business growth demands, volunteer work and having enough time for myself was a struggle. But every time I stepped on a golf course, it would force me to slow down, smell the roses and enjoy getting to know the people I was playing golf with. Playing a full round was difficult to do more than five times a summer, but getting out for a quick nine hole round was very doable. I only played recreational, casual golf and never kept score.

My competitive golf nature and love of teaching was revitalized when I discovered the sport of long drive. I remember my first long drive experience very well. I saw an ad in the paper for a local qualifier for the world long drive championships at a driving range near my house. When I was playing tour golf my driving distance was always long, so I thought hey why not? I hit a long ball, I should try this long drive thing.

I showed up to the range with my full set of golf clubs, paid my money and began warming up. After a few minutes I looked around and realized that everyone else was banging driver after driver - in fact, they had a whole bag full of just drivers! Music was blaring and people were talking excitedly and having fun. Where was I? Who were these people and what had they done with my sport? Instead of playing on a golf course, in long drive, you drive balls as far as you can within a marked area known as the 'grid.' You have six chances to land in the grid, and obviously, you are trying to hit your ball farther than anyone else.

I did well that day and advanced through the qualifying stages to make it to the world championships later that year. I loved the relaxed feeling of being able to swing a driver as fast as I could with no repercussions if a couple of them went wayward. I liked the adrenaline, the rush, the noise – I was hooked! And yes, I have a bag full of drivers now and have had the good fortune to win national and international championships.

However, my true passion with golf is the ability to mentor and teach women how to use golf to further their careers, deepen their relationships with friends and family and help support their communities. After teaching women how to swing a club for years, I realized that it is not enough. To feel confident to host or join another person on a golf course, you need to feel confident that you know how to be a good playing partner and how to manage your own emotions. Whether you want to entertain clients, participate in charity tournaments or you want to get to know your boss better, *Smashing The Grass Ceiling* is about opening up the game so you can take advantage of all the benefits that golf can provide.

I am often asked how I find the time to do all the things I do. How am I able to run a business, support my family, sit on committees and boards and volunteer in my community? I used to joke that I was starting a petition to increase the number of hours in a day to 28! What would I do with extra hours in the day? My answer used to be "work." Now my answer is "spend more time with people." As a mother of two teenagers, the opportunity to spend time with my kids without their faces stuck in their cell phones is precious. In your current busy lives, imagine if you spent more dedicated quality time with someone without any interruptions. If that someone was a potential client, a donor, an employer or a family member, imagine the opportunities gained from spending this time with them.

Do not let the misconceptions about golf or your insecurities stop you from realizing the amazing benefits that this game can bring to you. I strongly believe that women can do a better job at taking advantage of golf to build meaningful relationships in all aspects of their lives. *Smashing The Grass Ceiling* reframes traditional golf preconceptions and teaches strategies to make the game easier to play, take less time and therefore be an effective business tool. So, come and be a "Smashing Golfer" with me! Learn the strategies outlined in this book to take on the game with confidence so that you can build your networks, strengthen your relationships and advance your career.

CHAPTER 1

WHY GOLF IS A GREAT BUSINESS TOOL

Golf has always been a very effective way to do business. Where else can you have three to five hours of uninterrupted quality time with other people? Are you spending that entire time talking business? No, but you are building the foundation that will inevitably lead to better business relationships and hopefully lasting friendships. You do this by sharing stories, learning about each other's history, and making memories on the course that you can talk about for years. Yes, you can do this at a business lunch as well, but when you take a person outside their normal environment and put them in a much more casual setting, they become more receptive to you. *Playing a round of golf is an intimate, personal and effective way to build lasting personal and professional relationships.*

There are scarcely any instances nowadays where we can get a few focused, uninterrupted hours with someone. Golf gives us that glorious opportunity to spend quality time with other humans in a setting that promotes restoration and creativity. We will always have better clients, suppliers, board members, committee members and neighbours if we spend time and get to know each other without distractions.

While some men may be anxious to bring clients on the course, most have figured out how to fake confidence while they build up their golf experience. Many of the women I have taught are so self-conscious about playing with other people that they never use the game for business. I get that. When we golf, we put ourselves out there for everyone to see. Our mis-hits can't be hidden from view and anyone who has ever played golf knows that you can't hit a good shot every time. Most women will only do something if they are already fairly good at it, whereas the men I know are more apt to 'fake it till they make it!' So when an opportunity comes around to go to a golf tournament, many women make an excuse not to participate, while men take the opportunity presented. This results in women staying at the office, and doing a fabulous job, while our counterparts are out there having fun and more importantly, making the connections. I am here to tell you that you do not need to be a great golfer in order to use golf for business.

I will hammer this point home over and over again. It's not about being the best golfer. It's not about having the lowest score. *The ability to swing a golf club and hit a ball is not as important as the ability to manage the nuances and emotions of the game and the culture that surrounds it.* And there is not a woman that I know who doesn't inherently have the skills to recognize and handle the emotional subtleties in any situation. It's why more women should be in leadership, and it's why more women should be board members. We bring a different perspective to any situation. Managing a round of golf seems trivial in the grand scheme of things doesn't it? Make it through this book and you'll never be hesitant to play with anyone ever again.

Ditch the guilt and make time for golf

Golf has always been seen as an elitist luxury game and a privilege to play, so how do we take the time to play golf with all the pressures of work and life? For me, the issue was not as much time. I believe I can find the time to do something I really want to do. It was more the guilt. Yes, that age old feeling that seems to be passed down from generation to generation of women! Every time I was presented with the opportunity to golf, my first emotion was guilt for leaving my family to play or leaving my staff to handle things because I was out on the golf course. I squandered so many early business building opportunities. When I focused on playing golf to build and strengthen my relationships, I saw the value to my business. While I can't say the guilt is totally gone, it is certainly offset by the strong strategic connections and networks that the game has offered me. Pay attention to the men out there and when they go golfing. Most are golfing during the work day so that they can have their weekends with their families. If you are using golf as a business tool, then play golf during business hours. Don't feel guilty for taking the time to focus on your career and deepen your relationships.

Don't let preconceived notions stop you

While there are more women playing golf than ever, we are still a minority. Whether we like it or not, golf's history has been built on a long standing culture of sexism and you may face it when you step onto the course. Whether it's jokes about women golfers, the ridicule when men don't hit past the ladies tees, or the age old acronym about golf - Gentlemen Only Ladies Forbidden.

I cannot tell you the number of times I have showed up to the first tee paired with men I don't know, and I see the look of disappointment when they see me, "oh great we're playing with a woman." Of course, once I play a few holes, their moods change to "oh great, we're being out hit by a woman!" I'm a former pro and I still face the prejudice that women initially feel when playing. Whether we like it or not, we still feel like we have to try extra hard to prove ourselves out there. Remember: you are amazing in the boardroom and confident in your professional lives and I bet you work with men all the time. If you can handle those situations in your work life, then you can learn the knowledge and strategies you need to play golf confidently with anyone in any situation.

It's easy to make an excuse to avoid doing something difficult. Nowhere will you hear me say that golf is an easy game to play, because it's not. It takes years of practice to become competent. The good news is that there are plenty of ways to get better at playing. Come to one of my clinics or golf schools. Call me or one of the other amazing golf instructors out there. We can help you lower your score. But to use golf strategically and with confidence, you need insider knowledge about culture, etiquette and rules, and you need the tools to manage your own emotions. This book will get you out there with confidence to smash that grass ceiling and use golf to build strong sustainable relationships.

Marlane's story: *"The friendships that I've made on the golf course have lasted for decades. You cannot be a golfer if you do not have a sense of humour, an even temper and a respect for the rules of fair play. When I entered a male dominated profession it was my ability to play golf that assisted in my acceptance and built a strong foundation that lasted for over 30 years.*

I have spent quality time with my son on the golf course. We have had our best conversations and shared our hopes and dreams while spending our time together on the course. I cherish these times and know that we have many more to share. The benefits are so numerous to me ranging from the actual physical activity, time spent with good friends and family to the sense of satisfaction from making (even) that one great shot.

In today's society it is very difficult for many adults to find the time for themselves as their family is the priority but the benefits of golf are worth the time spent. You do not have to be great at the game but the game is what is great for you."
Marlane Robertson.

CHAPTER 2

GOLF EQUIPMENT

I have been teaching golf formally and informally for the last 20 years and the questions I am always asked are about equipment. This is a testament to the Golf Channel and club manufacturer's brilliant marketing. My students want to know if this club or that brand will make their game better. Should they buy this bag or those kinds of shoes? *While equipment absolutely matters, you don't need to spend a fortune to get started.* In this next section I will give you advice on what essential equipment you should have in your golf bag. I'll keep it simple and tell what you really need to know, not what the advertisers want you to hear. If you already have clubs feel free to skip to the next chapter.

Golf clubs - should you buy or rent?

First and foremost you need to figure out how committed you are to playing golf before you know whether you want to buy new or used clubs, or if you would rather just rent clubs when you need them. If your intention is to learn the game and play regularly with friends, family or for networking then, yes, you should buy your own clubs. If you are only going to play once or twice a year then rent clubs from the golf course. A lot of people don't consider this option, but it makes a lot of sense if you are not playing regularly. By renting you'll be playing with newer clubs than the ones you bought on a whim and have been sitting in your garage taking up space!

The other thing to remember is you don't have to buy clubs before your first golf lesson. Remember you are just testing out whether you like the game or not, so don't put the cart before the horse and go out and spend a bunch of money on clubs. Let your instructor know that you don't have clubs and they will arrange some for you to use. Once you have taken some lessons, decide if you like the game enough to spend a few hundred dollars on clubs, and then invest.

If buying used - make sure they are appropriate

I am all about a deal, and if a good set of used clubs comes your way, I say go for it - but make sure they are the right clubs for you. I've seen way too many women start out playing with hand me down men's clubs. Please, please, *please* play with women's clubs! The technology in golf clubs is based around the concept of swing speed, club weight and shaft flex all of which relate to strength. ***Men's clubs are too heavy and stiff for most women to hit easily or effectively.*** On top of that, technological advances in golf clubs are enormous and any set of clubs over five years old will not be as easy to hit as the newer ones, so please keep all of that in mind.

If buying new - get a starter set

In my opinion, if you take the time for lessons and want to use golf as a business tool, then invest in new clubs. But don't jump out and buy the shiniest, most technologically advanced set from the sales person at the golf store. If you are new to the game, the idea is to underspend on your first set. All you need is an easy to hit starter set which should cost around $400.

What's in a set of golf clubs?

A full set of golf clubs consist of 14 clubs and four different kinds of clubs: irons, hybrids, woods and a putter (don't worry, there is a chart in the appendix that goes over all of this.) The irons are numbered in order (most sets will have 5, 6, 7, 8, and 9 irons) along with two wedges: the pitching wedge (PW) and the sand wedge (SW). They are ordered based on length and loft. A 5 iron goes further than a 9 iron because it is longer, but it has less loft so it won't go as high. The wedges are your shortest clubs. Therefore, if you want to hit a short high shot you would take a higher number iron or one of the wedges.

The clubs with the big heads in a set are referred to as woods because they used to be made of wood like my original set of Patty Berg's when I was 10. Now they are made of a metal composite. You can get woods in a variety of lofts and lengths as well, the most common being a 5 wood, 7 wood and a Driver. Just like the irons, a 5 wood is longer than a 7 wood and a driver is the longest club in your bag, so theoretically it should go the farthest.

Hybrids are the latest addition to the family of golf clubs and as the name implies, they look like a cross between an iron and a wood. When I was a tour golfer more than 20 years ago, hybrids didn't exist, but boy my life would have been easier if they had been because they are much easier to hit. Hybrids are also commonly referred to as rescue clubs because you can use them in all kinds of tricky situations on a course when you need to 'rescue' your shot!

You only need seven clubs to start

The rules of golf allow you to carry 14 clubs in your bag. Personally, I think for a beginner, 14 clubs is way too much and leads to confusion. All you need to start out with are seven clubs: a driver, a 5 wood, a 5 hybrid, a 7 and 9 iron, a sand wedge and a putter. This will give you all the tools you need while keeping your budget under control. Invest in golf lessons as opposed to buying an expensive set of clubs.

Learning a golf swing with the wrong clubs can instill a lot of bad swing habits early on which will be hard to break. Give yourself the best chance for success by ensuring your clubs are appropriate.

Stand bags or cart bags

Usually a starter set of clubs will come with a bag, but for your general knowledge there are essentially two types of bags: stand bags and cart bags. A stand bag is designed for people to carry their clubs while walking a course. They tend to be lighter and smaller and will have fold out legs to 'stand' the bag while you take your shot. They come with suspension straps for you to wear your bag like a back pack. A cart bag is designed to be put on a cart or a pull/push cart. They are bigger, heavier and have more room to put things.

> Far's Tip: - I try and walk a course when I can, but I will always take a pull cart. If the course is hilly or long, I'll take a driving cart. Whenever I am playing golf and I see people carrying their own bag I am always in admiration of their motivation to exercise. I'm strong enough to carry my own bag, but I don't really want to. I would much rather ride in a cart or take a pull cart and save my energy to use in conversation or swinging the club. If you are an avid bag carrier and you are reading this, please don't be offended, I have a lot of respect and admiration for you. I also grew up in a golf environment where I had a caddy to carry my bag for me, so I have been thoroughly spoiled! Decide how you want to move around on the golf course and then buy the most appropriate bag to suit your needs.

Golf shoes are important

I always recommend buying golf shoes. The plastic spikes or rubber treads on the bottom of them help you grip the ground when you swing. They are also helpful for walking up and down hills on wet grass. That being said, my mum has wide feet and finds it nearly impossible to find a pair of golf shoes that are comfortable for her. For the last 10 years she has been wearing running shoes on the golf course and it suits her fine.

Like everything else, there's no need to overspend, simply find a pair that are comfortable the minute you put them on your feet.

Use ladies balls

Now I know you have walked into a golf store and noticed about 50,000 different kinds of golf balls for sale. While a lot of it has to do with marketing, there are some basic guidelines. Golf balls are designed on the principles of compression. How hard you swing the club will determine if you want a 'soft' or 'hard' ball. I highly recommend that women play with ladies' balls unless you have a really strong swing. They are softer and easier to hit and you'll want every advantage out on the course as you learn to play! Finally, a new ball flies further than an old one so don't be afraid to use those shiny new balls you bought.

Get a glove

Yes, you'll need one, so pick up a couple when you are at the golf store of your choice. Your glove is usually worn on just one hand (but you might want its mate if it's wet or cold out). If you are a right-handed golfer, the glove goes on your left hand and vice versa for the left-handed golfer. For a right-handed golfer the club sits in the palm of the left hand, so having a glove on limits the formation of calluses or blisters. It will also help keep your grip dry on hot sweaty days. Golfers usually wear their glove on all shots, but some prefer to putt without a glove so they remove it when putting only.

Doesn't matter what kind of tee you use

So you've made it to the tee section of the store and you are overwhelmed, right? Yes, tees come in all colours, shapes and sizes! It is a good idea to have a few tees of different heights in your bag as you figure out how high you like the ball teed up. Outside of that, you'll just need to experiment with different types and see what you like best. What you will need are plenty of them in your bag as they often break or get lost after a shot. I particularly like the Tornado Tee because not only does it look amazing, it has great technology that makes it feel like there is no resistance when my driver hits it.

Keep a divot repair tool handy

When playing ensure that you carry a divot repair tool to fix any marks you make on the green. We will talk about this again in the etiquette section later on. It doesn't matter which type of divot tool you use as long as you use one...all the time! Learn how to repair pitch marks and then go out there and look like a pro fixing the green. It is a surefire way to impress your playing partners!

Make your mark

A marker is placed on the green to mark the position of your ball. This allows you to lift your ball whether to move it out of the way of other players or to clean it. You can use any kind of marker you want. The little snap on your golf glove, a plastic marker many courses hand out for free, coins or a fancy branded one you will mostly likely get for Christmas now that you've taken up the game!

You will need a towel

Every bag needs a small towel hanging off it. They are usually sold with a clip for you to attach it to your bag. Trust me, you will use it more than you can imagine. You'll wipe your clubs free of wet grass, dirt and sand regularly. You'll also use it to dry off your hands when it's hot, if they are covered with sunscreen or if you've just opened a cold sweating drink!

> Far's Tip: Before you start your round, wet the bottom half of your towel so that it is easier to clean your ball and your clubs.

Golf equipment summary

Frankly, you can go totally overboard on purchasing golf equipment so please underspend at the beginning and wait to make major purchases when you have a better idea of what you want or need. Remember when it comes to clubs, you only need these seven clubs to get started:

- ☐ Driver

- ☐ 5 wood

- ☐ 5 hybrid

- ☐ 7 and 9 iron

- ☐ Sand wedge

- ☐ Putter

If you go to my website: www.farsamji.com, I have put together a starter set of clubs and equipment for the *Smashing the Grass Ceiling* program that is available to take all the guesswork out of getting started. Please don't go overboard with spending too much money on golf equipment right off the bat. Invest the money in lessons instead.

Caroline's Story: "*I started playing as a young sales professional because my job required me to network by playing in many golf tournaments. I decided if I wanted to enjoy golf I needed to invest in lessons and equipment to learn the game and feel more confident. I really believe that women in business need to take up the game as our male counterparts certainly do not think twice about missing work for a golf game to build a stronger client relationship or play*

in a tournament! In addition having the right equipment really makes a difference.

My advice to women starting to play the game is to start playing and understand that golf takes time and commitment to see improvement but even if you join a ladies league and golf once a week that is better than nothing. You will see improvement but most of all have fun and be confident! Enroll in annual Golf clinics customized for women– that is a real motivator and so much fun!" Caroline Johnson

CHAPTER 3

GOLF LESSONS

Becoming a Smashing golfer focuses on managing the game and your emotions irrespective of your actual ability to shoot a good score. Of course, you'll also want to be able to play the game better as well! I haven't met many people who don't want to be better at something! In order to do that, you'll need lessons and you'll need to practice. It's as simple (and as difficult) as that! In this section I'll go over everything you need to know to get yourself set up with lessons. Before we start, I will tell you unequivocally that you must take golf lessons in person before you venture out on the golf course. **Do not rely on your spouse's advice, YouTube videos, books or just winging it.** It will be a long, slow, frustrating journey if you go that route. I'm not saying you won't eventually figure it out, but you can get there a million times easier and faster if you take lessons from a qualified pro.

Taking lessons is like a continuing education course

The question is: what holds so many women back from taking lessons? The answer is similar to why woman are not using golf to further their careers: it's because taking lessons is intimidating. Face it, you have worked long and hard in your professional lives to gain the respect of your peers, to be taken seriously and to be seen as an equal in the workplace. It's hard to do something new that you also know is difficult and that will make you look and feel not very accomplished for the first little while. It takes confidence to learn a new skill in front of other people. On top of that, it's hard to know where to find lessons and then make time to invest in them. Trust me, the better you can play the game, the more fun it becomes and then you can spend less time worrying about how to play and more time on relationship building.

> Far's tip: Think of golf lessons as a continuing education course. Members of most professional associations are required to take a minimum amount of courses to maintain their certifications. When you don't feel confident about a task at work and you know it could benefit your career, you take a course to learn it. So, take golf lessons to acquire a skill that can enhance your business and help you build meaningful relationships and networks.

You have to like who you take lessons from

Golf lessons are offered at most golf courses, driving ranges and indoor golf training facilities. I recommend finding a place that is convenient to your home or work so that you give yourself the best chance of success to get there. I'd also check out private courses to see if they offer lessons to the public. These are not well advertised usually, but a phone call to ask is never a bad idea. Many private courses see giving lessons to non-members as a way of attracting new potential members to their club.

Choosing the right location to take your lessons may also depend on the type of instructor at each facility. When looking for a teaching pro, go to your network first. Put the word out asking if anyone has a golf instructor they would recommend in their area, much like you would do if you were looking for a tradesperson or a contractor. Referrals are always the first place to start.

You probably also want to give some thought as to whether you want to take lessons from a man or a woman depending on your comfort level. I have taken lessons from men and women and I've taught both. Ultimately the most important thing is that you are comfortable with the person you are working with.

When you find someone, your first step is to request a phone or email consultation or a brief five minute meeting. This initial meeting is an important way for you to gauge whether or not you like them. You have to at least like the person that is teaching you, and if they rub you the wrong way or your personalities clash from the very beginning, then you are never going to learn well! When people contact me for lessons, I always suggest they take one lesson (or a group lesson) with me first. Don't commit to a package until you try the person out. You may have to go through a couple of instructors till you find the right mix of experience, teaching style and personality.

You need a minimum of five lessons

At your first lesson, your instructor should have a conversation with you about your goals, expectations, previous golf history, and whether or not you have any injuries that may limit your ability to swing the club. Your goal could be simply to take a lesson so that you don't feel inadequate at the yearly corporate golf event, or it could be to take a few lessons so you can improve a particular part of your game, like driving. Whatever your goals and expectations are, communicate them to your instructor so they can design the best program for you.

If you are a beginner you should take a minimum of five lessons to begin with. Why five? Well, frankly, there is a lot to learn. During the first five lessons I usually cover basic swing mechanics, how to stand, how to hold the club, how to make the swing and the attributes of the different types of clubs as they relate to the short distance game and the long distance game.

Far's tip - After your five introductory lessons, ask your instructor to take you out on a golf course for a playing lesson. Golf is one of the few games where you practice and play in different locations. Practice happens on a driving range or at an indoor facility hitting into a screen. You actually play the game on a golf course. There is a big difference between practicing and playing which makes the transference of information quite challenging. A playing lesson on a golf course will give you the knowledge you need to apply your practise and actually play the game itself.

It takes a lot of practice to be a good golfer

If you've never played before and you're taking lessons for the first time, you can pretty much expect to not be very good at the game after your first five lessons! I'm not saying this to discourage you, but more to frame your expectations. It will take a lot of practice to be a capable golfer. It will take that and many more rounds to become good at it, and it can take years and years to become great at it. It's what makes the game so addictive. You can be a great golfer and go out and shoot a bad round one day and be awesome the next. I joke about the fickle golf gods, but it's true, even the pros can't shoot lights out every round. Lessons will provide you with the tools you need to know how and what to practice.

All the tools in the world will mean nothing if you don't take the time to play and practise! In my experience, most people do not practise enough in between and after their lessons, mostly because it's intimidating to show up at a driving range by yourself as a beginner let alone to know what and how to practise. Lessons will give you the basic information you need to get started but you have to be able to put in the time to learn how to apply what you have been taught. When you practise between your lessons, you can give your instructor some feedback on how it felt to hit when they weren't around to correct you. Also, it's harder to remember things when your instructor isn't standing beside you reminding you!

> Far's tip: When you get to the driving range or indoor practice facility, don't hit any more than 75 balls or spend longer than 20 minutes practising. You serve yourself better to put in a few short sessions before your first round of play as opposed to one or two long practise sessions. I would much rather you spend several short bursts of concerted practise than stand out there and beat balls. Use your time more effectively by practising for 20 minutes at a time and then actually playing a round of golf.

How to practise

My practise routine always starts with a few back and shoulder stretches to prevent injury, and then a few practise swings without the ball to warm up the motion in the correct plane. Next I begin with some short distance shots with my wedge starting with half swings and progressing to full swings. From there I move to my 7 iron for a few shots, then my hybrid or fairway wood and finally I hit about 10-15 drives with my driver. I always save five balls to finish my practice sessions with five more chip shots. Just like with anything you do in life, the more you practise the better you get, so keep it short and manageable and give yourself the chance to succeed. Your golf instructor should also give you some tips on how to practise when you take your lessons.

The best practise is to play

I am not a believer in hitting balls on the driving range excessively. There is a place for the range, absolutely, but no more than 20 minutes at a time in my opinion. Instead I encourage you to find opportunities to play the game with friends as you gain confidence. Join a ladies league and play regularly to build up your skills. There are many opportunities to play the game via charity tournaments and these make great venues to learn the game and feel capable before taking out clients for a golf game.

Golf lessons summary

I still take golf lessons regularly because there is always a need to have someone else's eye helping me see what I can't in my own swing. The best golfers in the world take lessons so please don't stop after one season of golf. Think of it like a tune up to help you get better, like a regular massage to keep your muscles loose, or an oil change to keep your car running. If you are looking at golf to help you build your relationships, invest in some lessons and then play the game.

- ☐ Find an instructor you connect with

- ☐ Take a minimum of five lessons to start

- ☐ Practise for 20 minutes in between lessons

- ☐ Ask for a playing lesson

- ☐ Get out there and play

A good instructor will give you a goal to work towards and once you have reached it, it will be time for a new one. Let me remind you one last time - after you take lessons you absolutely need to practise and play regularly! So dig your heels in, get out there, enjoy yourself and play!

Michelle C's Story: "I started playing because a few of my University friends were into it and it was a fun way to hang out and get some exercise (there may have been beer involved after too!) I always liked the combination of athleticism and thought that goes into every golf round, and once I started to play better I really fell in love with the game. It's something

my husband and I can plan trips around, or just go for 9 holes on a Friday evening. We walk the course, talk along the way, and it's something we'll be able to do together even as we age.

Professionally, I notice that I'm 100% confident any time the topic of golf comes up. I'm a PGA/LPGA geek so I can hold my own in conversations around Fedex Cup or Solheim Cup or the latest news on Tiger or Rory. I can be 'one of the guys' if it's warranted. Admittedly I don't have many women friends who are as into golf as I am, so I usually am playing with my husband and other men.

The biggest deterrent to getting out on the golf course 'before lessons' was the frustration levels I'd feel because the ball rarely went where I wanted it, which makes for a tiring and unsatisfying round. The most consistent part of my game was inconsistency. Lessons (and regular practice) changed all that for me. When the ball starts to go straight and you start hitting fairways and greens in regulation it's a whole new game. And I LOVE it. Lessons will make a world of difference with confidence and enjoyment of the sport.

You don't have to be super strong to hit a good golf ball, so women can do it very well even if they don't feel like they are 'athletes'. So much of it is technique, and with a good instructor (and regular focused practice) the game is so much more fun! Don't let your spouse or partner be your golf coach. My husband is a good golfer but he doesn't know the best ways to teach a proper swing. Save your relationship. Hire a pro. The game has to be fun first. If my game is imploding (it happens) I will stop keeping score and just focus on making the next shot as good as possible." Michelle Cederberg.

CHAPTER 4

KNOWING YOUR WAY AROUND THE GOLF COURSE

One of the main reasons why more women don't use golf as a business tool is because the golf course and clubhouse itself are mysterious and intimidating places with so many rules and customs. Some have dress codes and others give you the feeling that you don't belong there from the moment you set foot inside the entrance. Did you know that there are 30,000 courses worldwide? Some will be palaces built in honour of the sport and others will be … let's say, more functional. No matter where you play, they will all have the same fundamental features.

The point of this chapter is to walk you through the process of arranging a game for yourself, either alone or with others. I will take you through all the areas of the golf course and teach you what to say and do so you will always look and feel like you belong. I'll teach you how to make a tee time, what questions to ask when calling the pro shop and what happens from arriving at the course to hitting your first shot. Some of you may not be ready to play the game yet, and will only play in charity or fun tournaments, but they all involve the same areas of the golf course. The more you know, the more confident you will be. If you know your way around the clubhouse and pro shop feel free to skip this chapter!

Call the pro shop to make a tee time

To make a tee time, you call the pro shop at the golf course. The conversation should sound like this:

"Hi, this is the pro shop, how can I help you?"

"Hi, I'd like to make a tee time for 11:30am for next Tuesday for four people. Do you have time available?"

See, simple! The pro shop will check their schedule and let you know if there is availability and if not, they will offer you other possible times. It's just like making an appointment with your dentist, but way more fun.

Don't be afraid to ask questions when making your tee time. Find out when the course is busy. Ask if there is a dress code. Find out what their cancellation policy is. If you are playing with only one other partner, find out if they will place another twosome with you. If you are taking a key client or playing for the first time with your boss, you can never have too much information!

Drive to the bag drop first

When you arrive at a course there will usually be a sign that says 'bag drop.' Follow the signs and drive to the front of the clubhouse next to a bag stand to place your clubs in. Courses do this as a courtesy so you don't have to carry your clubs all the way from your car in the parking lot. Fancier clubs will have employees who will take your clubs out of your car for you and organize them onto a driving cart or pull cart for your game.

Once you park, your next move is to head into the pro shop. You will find most pro shops look more like stores than places to organize tee times. Wind your way through the racks of golf shirts and hats and head to the desk. The pro shop's key job is managing the scheduling for the course. When I worked in a pro shop, new golfers would walk in with a look of terror in their eyes. You know that deer in the headlight look of, "What do I do? Where do I go?" Nine times out of ten, they would avoid the desk altogether and go wander around the store because it was way more comfortable to pretend to shop than to engage in a conversation about golf!

Once you've made a tee time, arrived at the course and dropped off your clubs, stride confidently into the pro shop, right up to the desk and check in just like you would do at the dentist's office. The pro shop will confirm your tee time and ask you to pay for the round. Lastly, they'll give you a receipt that you'll need to show on the course before you start, so keep it in a handy place!

Get there early

If the course you are playing has practice facilities, I can't encourage you enough to get there early and warm up a little (10-15 mins) to get your jitters out. Trust me, we all get them. You will feel a million times more confident hitting your first tee shot if you have had the opportunity to hit a few balls beforehand. I will take you through a simple warm up routine for the driving range a little later in the book.

It's also a good idea to be at the starting hole 15 minutes before your tee time, so plan ahead. You'll be met there by the 'starter.' Their job is to regulate timing and to give you information about the course before you start. They can help you determine what tee blocks you should play from, how long it should take you to play the course (pace of play) and they'll let you know other important things like where the bathrooms are and if there is a drink cart out on the course. The starter will also ask to see your payment receipt.

The most important reason for getting to the course early, however, is to stay organized and calm. If you are rushed you will be flustered. Have you ever been late to the airport? You know that panicked feeling as you break every traffic law so you can get there on time? Trust me, if you arrive for your tee time with seconds to spare, it will affect your game and your frantic energy will affect the people you are playing with. Be prepared. Warm up. Be ready to go in a cool calm state!

Start with 9 holes

The absolute worst thing a new golfer can do is play 18 holes! Seriously, don't do that to yourself. It will not be fun. If your first exposure to golf is a charity tournament and it's an 18 hole event, that's different and we will talk later in the book about how to manage that. If you are looking to play to build relationships, start with 9 holes and build up your stamina to play 18. Your playing partners will thank you for this because they probably aren't in 18 hole shape either and no one wants to be set up to fail! Nine holes will take about two or two and a half hours to play and it's the perfect length of time to get to know someone better and still get other work done in the day.

Think of this as an audition. It's long enough to relax and enjoy time with someone, but not too long so that you both get tired, distracted, and too caught up emotionally with how your game is going. This is key if you are a beginner, or are playing with a beginner. It's easier for everyone to have fun on the course if they're not exhausted. It also shows respect for their time and yours. Once you've had a bunch of games under your belt and you know you are playing with seasoned golfers, then start to organize full 18 hole games.

Take a cart if you need to

I have walked plenty of golf courses and carried my own bag on tour when I couldn't afford a caddy and we weren't allowed carts. It is a truly horrible feeling to be huffing and puffing after climbing a huge hill to then have to settle your heart rate and hit a shot across a huge pond!

Yes, walking is great exercise and one of the many benefits of the game, but many of today's courses are long and hilly and you just won't have any fun if you are exhausted. If you are certain you want to walk the course, I recommend a pull cart so that you aren't carrying your clubs on your back. Once you work up the stamina and can carry your own bag and walk, it is a great way to get a workout in! Ideally though, riding in a cart with your guest affords you a wonderful opportunity to talk shop, life or just share a joke or two.

Women usually play from the forward tee blocks

The 'tee deck' is a raised area marked by two coloured tee blocks on either side of the deck. This is where you play your first shot from, or your 'tee shot.' Which tee blocks you should play from is determined by how good a golfer you are, or think you are. While I rarely see women playing from the wrong tee deck, men notoriously choose a tee deck too far back for their game. Not only does it affect their score, but it slows down the game.

I cannot tell you how many people play from the back tees when they really should be playing from the more forward options. You know who you are out there - stop doing it! Unless you hit a long ball, most women play from the forward tees. There is no shame in playing from the forward tees in golf, they are there for a reason - to equalize the game and give everyone a chance to play together while still playing at different ability levels.

Know how to identify your ball

As soon as the starter gives the go ahead it's time to hit the first tee shot. All golf balls have a brand name and number on them. It's a good idea to call out your ball to your playing partners so that everyone knows whose ball is whose when they are out there side by side. I would say, "I am playing a Callaway 3," for example. If you play a common ball type, it doesn't hurt to mark your ball with a sharpie to help identify it.

The first shot is always the hardest

The first shot on the first hole (your tee shot) is usually the most nerve wracking because it feels like everyone is watching and you don't want to mess it up. This doesn't just apply for women. Many guys are just as jittery on their first tee shot of the day. Take a few practise swings, a few deep breaths and remember you are out there to make relationships. They don't care if you hit a bad shot, so why should you? But fear not, I will give you some tips for how to manage the first tee jitters later in the book.

Knowing your way around the golf course summary

Okay I've got you covered from booking your tee time to your first shot of the round. While this may be old hat for some of you, fancy clubhouses and pro shops can be intimidating. Follow my lead and you'll look like you've done this a million times before. Your boss or potential client will have no clue that you are new at using golf as a business tool. I don't know many people who don't like to gather as much information as they can before doing something new. The more you know, the more confident you will be!

Emily's Story: *"I started playing golf for business and fell in love with the sport. Unlike all of the other team sports I played, this was a zen sport and I realized I could channel my yoga-like moments in nature while competing internally to be the best I possibly can be, one stroke at a time.*

Building relationships professionally and personally has cemented the value of this sport. The time it takes to play golf, creates a foundation where one cannot hide their true personality and it is the ultimate interview. The individuals I have come to respect while playing golf demonstrated honesty, integrity, grit, compassion and empathy.

My advice to other women is patience and practice. Adjust the sport so you have fun as you get better. Remember every stroke is not the pursuit of perfection and enjoy the experience regardless of how many strokes it took you to get to the cup. It is a sport you can grow old with and you can play with anyone in the world: the great equalizer. All you need is a positive spirit, enthusiastic energy and a smile (for me, a couple dozen golf balls per round, lol.)" Emily Phillips Teh

CHAPTER 5

GOLF ETIQUETTE

One of the main reasons golf is intimidating is because there are so many unwritten rules of behaviour. This is called 'golf etiquette' and trust me, get this wrong and it will grate on your playing partner's every last nerve. It's mortifying when you are on the golf course and someone tells you that you're standing in the wrong spot, especially if that person is your boss, a client, or worse, a potential new client. Get etiquette right and people will be so impressed they won't care about your score!

While I could write an entire book about golf behaviour, we are just going to focus on the key details of proper etiquette on the golf course. I'm going to cover what I think are the most important things to know, and before you realize it, you will look and feel like you know exactly what you are doing.

I grew up in a very traditional golf environment where everyone followed the rules and etiquette was jammed down my throat from the first time I picked up a club. Yes, I agree it's important and that it is part of the tradition of the game, but sometimes people can take it too far. I mean, seriously, some people need to play with blinders on and ear plugs in because even the slightest movement or sound bothers them. Learn and follow the etiquette suggestions I outline below, but please be reasonable and enjoy yourself out there without getting too hung up on the details.

I have divided this chapter into two sections: general etiquette for playing and then a specific section on etiquette for when you are on the green.

General etiquette

Ask where you should stand

While this may seem ridiculous to talk about, where you stand when your playing partners are hitting is actually really important. The rule of thumb is to stand facing the person hitting the ball so that their swing path and peripheral vision is clear. What I mean by this is if a person is teeing off aiming for 12 on a clock, you should stand at the equivalent of 3 o clock (if they are right handed). Some people will stand behind my back (or at 9 on the clock) where I can't see them. Personally, I don't like that because while I can't see you, I can sense you! It sounds ridiculous right? But it's true, if it bothers you, it will affect your shot.

Quite often I see people standing directly behind a person's backswing (or at 6 on the clock) and that will almost always distract a golfer unless you stand perfectly still. My friend Helen always makes it a point to ask the golfers she is playing with if they have a preference as to where they would like her to stand. This simple conversation at the start of the game helps alleviate any potentially embarrassing situations later on.

Be quiet!

This is probably the biggest pet peeve of any golfer in the world. So let me say this most emphatically - do not talk, cough, sneeze, laugh, sing, play an instrument or do a dance while someone is taking their shot. Seriously. Stand still and be quiet. This is a case of do unto others as you would like them to do unto you. Pay attention to when someone is going to swing and then settle. It's simple to do and your playing partners will love you for it!

Long drive events have music blaring all the time so I am used to playing with noise now, but this wasn't always the case. When I used to play pro golf, the simplest things would break my concentration. The swishing noise of rain pants during soggy rounds or worse still, the sound of people jingling their change in their pockets when I was trying to putt. This would drive me insane! Really, how ridiculous is that?

Humans are a funny bunch. What will bother one person, won't bother someone else. I say, hedge your bets. No one will ever get mad at you for standing still and keeping quiet while your partners hit.

Use common sense when driving a cart

One of the golf courses I worked at in my early days as a club pro had a pond named Mabel's Pond. Why you ask? Well Mabel had infamously driven her cart into the pond (which thankfully was only 1 foot deep.) While this happened long before I started working there, I'm sure that Mabel was having a blast on the golf course and wasn't paying attention to her cart!

Let me just start by stating the obvious. Carts are fun. There probably isn't a person in the world who doesn't love jumping into one and zipping around the course. However, if you have ever done any gardening in your life you can appreciate the amount of hours it takes to grow a perfect lawn. The grounds crew on a golf course work painstakingly to ensure their courses look pristine. They are usually there at 5 am working diligently so that everything is perfect for you when you arrive.

Just because you pay your greens fees it doesn't mean you can do anything you want on the course. Here we return to those 'unwritten rules.' It is every golfer's responsibility to be respectful of the course they are playing on.

Some cart fundamentals for you to know: NEVER drive on the tee decks or the greens. Every course will have 'cart exit' signs posted where they want you to exit the fairway. If you see short posts to prevent you from driving in or off the fairway, respect them and look for the access points the grounds crew want you to use. They do this so that they can manage damage to the grass from carts repeatedly driving over the same areas. When you are on the fairway, try and avoid low lying areas if you know the course is wet. You will often see cart tracks from someone else not paying attention.

Most importantly, be aware of your surroundings. Carts can tip over. I've seen it happen and people can get injured. So be smart about steep hills, know where the sand bunkers are, don't drive into hazard land or out of bounds areas, and look for signs regarding ground under repair. If the course is particularly wet, they may want you to be 'cart path only,' which means the carts can't go onto the fairway at all. Think of this as an excellent excuse for more exercise that day! But please ladies, if your ball lands far away from the cart path, guess at what clubs you might need and take a few with you to your ball. There is nothing (and I mean nothing) more annoying than waiting for someone to go back to their cart to get another club when their cart is parked far away from the ball!

In general, driving a cart requires some common sense and forward thinking. Pay attention to where the best place is to park when you are putting. It should be close to where you will be walking off the green after you finish the hole and not where your ball lands initially. And also please look around you. Make sure you park your cart in a position that other carts can pass by yours.

Finally I should mention the parking brake. All carts have a brake to slow down and stop the cart when you are driving. Once you stop, you should put the cart into 'park.' This will stop any embarrassing moments when you've gone to your ball and your cart starts moving on you. And trust me, we have ALL had that happen to us at some point or another. So when you are stopped, put the parking brake on. Hey, maybe that's what happened to Mabel?

Lowest score on the previous hole determines who hits first

Teeing off first is called having the 'honour' and the person with the best score on the previous hole (meaning lowest number of strokes to get the ball into the hole) earns the honour of hitting first. Then you continue to tee off in order of how people scored the previous hole. To some people this is a really big deal so be mindful before stepping up to take your shot. If you are playing with golfers who hit from different tee decks, it's obvious that the players teeing off furthest back should go first for safety reasons.

And if this all seems a bit much…well, it is. Frankly, if you are playing a casual round of non-competitive golf most people will play 'ready' golf which means if you are ready to go, get up there and hit it! We will talk about ready golf a lot more in a later section.

Watch everyone's ball

I was playing in a charity event with my brother and we got paired up with a real estate agent and a business consultant. It was a scramble format so the group of us teed off, decided which drive was best and then collected the rest of the balls to take to this position to shoot our next shot from. It's a common format for tournaments and I will cover it in more detail in the tournament section of the book.

In true networking fashion, by the third hole we had all shared what we do for a living and I was really intrigued by what the business consultant had to say. Both my brother and I were thinking expansion or franchising at the time and it seemed like a perfect fit for us to engage his services. We had been making a good connection on the golf course. (This, by the way, is the advantage of participating in charity tournaments. While you might not personally need the services of your playing partners, you probably know someone who will).

On the fourth hole, my brother and I both hit into the left rough while the other two went straight down the fairway. We went to go look for our balls and the real estate agent walked over to help us look. Not the business consultant, he went directly to his ball (which happened to be the best shot) and pulled out his cell phone to send a few texts. It bugged me, but I let it go and we found our balls and continued the game.

As we kept playing, I started noticing that the guy never helped look for anyone's ball. In fact he didn't even have a clue as to where the other balls were on the course other than his own. By the end of the round I was completely turned off by his oblivious, self-centred behaviour. He may have been a great talker about his services and how he could help us, but his actions on the golf course gave me insight into his true character and ruined any chance of me doing business with him. I will not do business with someone I don't like!

So please, please, please, make it your practice to watch everyone's shots so that you know where your own ball is, and can help look for your playing partner's balls if they go off the fairway. It's not easy to track the ball when it's hit, so it will take some practise. Use cues to help you remember the position of the ball. Like that red tree, or near that short flowering bush. Not only will they thank you for this, but you will come across as a thoughtful and attentive person. Isn't that just the kind of impression you want to make with potential clients or work colleagues? Actions have consequences, so keep your head in the game and be helpful.

Leave the course better than you found it

It's inevitable that when you swing your club you will eventually dig up some grass. This is called making a divot. If you have a powerful swing, you will make a divot almost every time you swing your club. While some of you might not make a divot on purpose, you will chunk out a piece of grass eventually. Either way, divots are an expected part of the game.

I bring this up because most women I play with are scared to hit the ground or are even upset when they make a divot. Don't be. The grounds crew have you covered. Simply grab the piece of turf you have ripped out, place it back in the hole and stamp your foot down on it. If it's more like a scar on the ground instead of a nice chunk of grass, grab the container of sand and seed mix that you will find on your cart and fill in the hole.

Now let's talk about sand. Bunkers are there to remind you that golf is a hard sport! The number one rule to remember is that you want to erase all trace of yourself in the bunker after you have left it. That's why you'll find rakes sitting beside the bunkers. When your ball goes in the sand, simply grab the nearest rake and bring it with you into the bunker. After you have hit your shot, use the rake to smooth the sand as you back yourself out. Once you are done with the rake, leave it outside the bunker, not blocking the entrance to it.

Greens etiquette

The green is at the end of the fairway where you will find the flag and the hole that you will putt your ball into. You will notice quickly that the green is also the most finely manicured part of the golf course and the most fragile. Just walking on the green can leave footprints and jumping or twisting can really chew it up. Even dropping your clubs or the flag down on the ground can mark up the green. So please be careful. The smoother the surface, the easier it is to putt for everyone.

Fix your pitch mark

When your ball lands on the green with enough speed, it will leave a small divot or pitch mark on the green. **While it is good etiquette to fix your own pitch marks, it is GREAT etiquette to fix any pitch marks you see on the green that some other oblivious or lazy golfer left before you.** Your pitch mark may be a fair distance away from your ball, so be sure to look for it on the green. You can easily get a little divot repair tool from the pro-shop or a golf store. Keep it handy in your pocket as you play.

There are many ways to fix a pitch mark but here is a simple method that I use. Your divot tool has prongs on the end of it. Insert the prongs into the grass at the rim of the mark as opposed to inside the depression made by the divot. Gently push the edges in towards the centre. Continue around the entire rim so that you are pushing the grass into the depression from all sides. Flatten by gently tapping the surface using the sole of your putter or your foot. If you fix your pitch mark right away the grass will recover quicker, leaving the green in great shape.

The person farthest from the hole putts first

Once everyone has their ball on the green, the first person to putt is the person farthest away from the hole. Simple right? But who goes first if you have a 40 foot putt and your playing partner has a 4 foot chip shot just off the green? Usually the person off the green will hit first simply because you want everyone on the green before you pull the flag. It's more efficient this way. It's a pain to have to remove the flag for your long putt and then put it back in for the short chip.

It is always good practice to ask the person chipping onto the green if they would like you to remove the flag for them or not. Don't assume one way or the other. Ask and you'll look like a rock star out there!

Put your marker behind your ball

The green is the only place on the golf course where you can pick up your ball if you are playing by the official rules of golf (when you play by 'Far's Rules', there are exceptions which I will outline later in the book.) What you need to know is that *before* you lift your ball, you must mark it. You can use a coin or an actual ball marker, it doesn't really matter. But what does matter is how you mark it - place the marker *behind* the ball (as determined by where the ball is in conjunction to the hole).

This is a simple thing, but trust me, if you put your marker beside or in front of the ball, people will grumble. I guarantee that one of your playing partners will point out that you are doing it wrong and you'll feel like an idiot.

It's good practice to always mark your ball on the green and pick it up, that way your ball isn't a visual distraction to others putting and you can clean your ball off to help it roll more smoothly. To replace your ball, put it down on the ground in front of your marker in the exact same spot, remove your marker and then putt.

You'll find that at some point in the game your ball will be in someone else's way. It's inevitable, but don't worry, once you mark your ball ask the other player if they want you to move your mark. Always ask because sometimes it looks like you will be in the way, but they might be aiming somewhere else. **It's the other player's responsibility to ask you to move your mark, but it is always good etiquette to ask.** Usually they will say the direction they want you to move it in (left or right of the original position). Whichever direction you move your marker, just make sure you move it back to the original position before you make your putt.

Do not step in the line of anyone's putt

Ladies read the next line very carefully please: DO NOT STEP IN THE LINE OF ANYONE'S PUTT!! Sorry, didn't mean to yell, but it's really that important. I said earlier that golf pushes people's buttons and this is a big one. A footprint on the green will act like a pothole for the ball as it is trying to roll smoothly into the hole. When approaching the green, pay attention to where everyone's ball is and walk around so as not to step on the line (or intended path) of their ball to the hole.

I have seen some people get fuming mad when their line is stepped on, and yes any reaction that extreme is unreasonable. However, some people need something to blame their bad putt on and I don't want it to be you! Imagine the image it sends to your boss or potential client. You want them to remember how much fun they had with you, not that you ruined their birdie putt. People can hang on to that for a very long time - irrational or not.

Watch for shadows

When playing in the afternoon, you'll need to pay attention to shadows. Whether it's your body or the pin, depending on the light, you can be casting a shadow on your playing partner's line. This makes it difficult for your partner to read the putt or to gauge distance. So just watch where you are standing and move if you need to.

The person whose ball is closest to the hole pulls the flag

When you are putting on the green, the flag (also known as the 'pin') must be pulled from the hole before the ball touches it. It is good practice to remove the flag once everyone's balls are on the green. The person whose ball is closest to the hole, and therefore last to putt, should pull the flag out of the hole. If that is you (nice shot!) ask the person farthest away from the hole if they can see the hole clearly and should you pull the flag or 'tend' it. If everyone can see the hole clearly from where they are, pull the flag and place it out of the way.

Tending the flag means that you hold on to the flag until the person farthest away starts their putt. It is meant as a courtesy so the player can see the hole better as they line up their shot. Once they have hit their ball, you pull the flag and put it somewhere out of the way. I'm going to say it again, because it's that important - *DO NOT STEP IN ANYONE'S LINE*. Make sure you know where the other balls or markers are and stand appropriately.

Finally, it's good practice to wait until everyone is on the green before starting to putt. Why? Because putting is hard and you can learn the slopes of the green by watching other people's putts, and more importantly, it's more fun if you play together. Similarly, you should wait on the green until everyone finishes putting. It's polite and shows good sportsmanship even if what you really want to do is throw your putter in the pond!

If you are the first person to finish putting then your reward is the job of managing the flag and replacing it in the hole after the last person putts. Make it your mission to always want to replace the flag. Not only will you be fun to play with, but your score will be a lot lower too!

Give a gimme, get a gimme

A 'gimme' is a short putt that your playing partners assume you will make so you don't have to hit it and can just pick up the ball. The term is from "will you give me that putt?" Usually 'gimmes' are inside a foot but if you're playing with me, my 'gimmes' can be several feet. I'm pretty generous! It's important to gauge with your group if 'gimmes' are ok with them.

'Gimme' etiquette is give if you get, so they should be shared equally. If someone gives you a 'gimme', look for opportunities on the green to return the favour. If you are staying true to your score then let your playing partners know and don't take any 'gimmes'. Hit every shot till you hear the ball bounce into the cup.

I have noticed that not everyone likes 'gimmes'. They want to play every shot because they are recording their score for their handicap or they like the practice or they want the satisfaction of finishing the hole. So please ask your group ahead of time if 'gimmes' are ok - it's always better to know instead of guessing. To give a 'gimme' to someone, the proper words to say are "given" or "that's a gimme" or "that's good." It's ok to be generous if you are playing a fun casual round of golf, just remember to count the stroke of the 'gimme' in your score.

Golf etiquette summary

Feeling overwhelmed by all the etiquette yet? This is why a lot of people give up on the game. But fear not, I have given you a crash course that will do you well in almost any golf game situation. That's the point of being a Smashing golfer. You can spend the entire round duffing shot after shot, but if you're paying attention and being respectful to the course and to your playing partners, people will always want to play a round with you.

People like to play golf with other people who understand how to play the game. It's as simple as that so please reread this section ten times if you need to. Follow these etiquette rules and you will be able to play golf with anyone and use the time out there to network and build solid, strong relationships.

Mary's Story: "My husband taught me how to golf in my 40's. I only took up the game so I could spend time with him, doing something he loved. Then we divorced and I was in trouble! He was the only one I was comfortable golfing with. I even made him pay for four players when we golfed so I wouldn't have to golf in front of anyone else.

I have my own little tricks. I don't keep score and I "tee" up all my hits, except when I use my pitching wedge or putter. I am afraid of hitting the club on the ground and hurting myself. Finally, last year, I decided that I love to golf and can actually hit a few fantastic balls. I now play the way I want to play, (always respecting course rules) and I golf with anyone who asks me. I don't put myself down, I just do my best and I love it!" Mary Dilly

CHAPTER 6

KNOWING THE RULES

(Co-written with Cory Ann Pond, PGA of Canada,
Level 2 Golf Canada Rules Official)

For the rules section of the book, I have enlisted the help of my good friend and level 2 Golf Canada rules official, Cory Ann Pond. I'm pretty good with the rules, but Cory is an expert and rules are, well, rules and it's important to understand them. I'm not a particular stickler about the rules because most of my rounds are non-competitive and recreational, however back in my pro days missing a rule could mean losing a stroke, and losing a stroke could mean losing money. Back then, every dollar I earned on the course was essential to being able to eat and pay for my hotel rooms!

What I've done in this section is try and identify a few of the key rules that you will encounter on a regular basis and give you the hard facts about what you are supposed to do. Whether you choose to follow these to the letter is up to you and your playing partners and whether you are scoring your round accurately or playing for fun.

In each section we will quote the actual rule so you can see the language used (cringe) and then Cory and I will translate it into language easier to understand and give you examples of how the rule is applied. The point of this section is to equip you with the knowledge you need to look confident out on the course and to help avoid some 'helpful' playing partner telling you what you are doing wrong on the course.

CORY: As of 2017 there are 34 rules in Golf Canada's Rules of Golf. However, there are only a handful of these rules that are actually necessary to know during a recreational round of golf. Remember that golf is a game and it's meant to be fun, so try not to let the rules interfere too much.

Tee Shot Rules

Rule 11-4. Playing from Outside Teeing Ground

*"If a competitor, when starting a hole, plays a ball from outside the teeing ground, he incurs a penalty of two strokes and must then play a ball from within the teeing ground."**

CORY: What this means is that when teeing up your ball on the tee decks, always play your tee shot from between the tee markers, never in front of them. Your tee shot can be played from behind the tee-markers but no more than two club-lengths behind. If you are ahead of the tee markers or too far back (more than 2 club lengths) then it is considered 'outside the teeing ground' and you are charged a 2 stroke penalty. Your ball must be in between the tee-markers, but your feet can be in front of or outside the tee-markers with no penalty.

FAR: Here's a little tip: Stand behind the tee markers and see where they are naturally aiming you. You will be surprised to see on how many holes the tee markers are actually facing you into the trees or a hazard. Most people just walk up and tee their ball in the middle between the two markers. Next time, look at where you want to aim and choose a nice flat spot for your tee!

Rule 11-3. Ball Falling off Tee

"If a ball, when not in play, falls off a tee or is knocked off a tee by the player in addressing it, it may be re-teed, without penalty." *

CORY: Has this ever happened to you? You tee up the ball, and then as you are getting settled in to take your swing, the ball falls off the tee, and your playing partners say "one" meaning that counts as a stroke. Well, it's not true, it's a joke, so don't fall for it!

If your ball falls off the tee or you knock it off when addressing the ball, there is no penalty and you can replace the ball and proceed to take your shot. So if they say "one" you can very quickly reply with, "not according to Rule 11-3!" (who's the joker now?!)

Rules when your ball is in a Hazard (water or sand)

FAR: What's a beautiful golf course without some water or sand? If you play golf you will likely donate a few balls to the water (as I do quite often) and you will hit your ball into the sand eventually! I mean, it would be a shame not to see the whole course if you are paying good money for your round, right? So it's important to know what to do when you get into the hazard.

Rule 26-1. Relief for Ball in Water Hazard

"If a ball is found in a water hazard or if it is known or virtually certain that a ball that has not been found is in the water hazard (whether the ball lies in water or not), the player may under penalty of one stroke:

Proceed under the stroke and distance provision of Rule 27-1 by playing a ball as nearly as possible at the spot from which the original ball was last played or

Drop a ball behind the water hazard, keeping the point at which the original ball last crossed the margin of the water hazard directly between the hole and the spot on which the ball is dropped, with no limit to how far behind the water hazard the ball may be dropped; or

As additional options available only if the ball last crossed the margin of a lateral water hazard, drop a ball outside the water hazard within two *club-lengths of and not nearer the hole than the point where the original ball last crossed the margin of the water hazard or a point on the opposite margin of the water hazard equidistant from the hole."* *

CORY: Phew - that's a lot of information! What it means is that if you wind up in the water you have four different options to play your next shot.

1) Play the ball from where it lies without penalty - This first option is quite simple, play it. If the ball is visible in the water and you feel like taking off your shoes and rolling up your pants you have the option to go into the hazard and swing away. (Probably not advisable in some courses in Florida that have alligators). But if you are going to play in the water you cannot 'ground your club' which means you can't let your golf club touch the water or the ground in preparation for your shot. So in essence, the club must hover.

    If you decide you don't want to lose your leg to the alligator, any of these options below will cost you a one stroke penalty.

2) Play the ball where you initially hit it from - for example, if you hit a ball from the tee deck into the water, you may hit another ball from the tee deck.

3) Drop a ball any distance behind the water hazard - In order to determine where to drop your ball, you have to imagine a straight line between the hole and where your ball last crossed into the water. Then you move backward as far behind the water hazard as you need to go to find a safe place to drop the ball.

4) Drop a ball within two club lengths of where your ball entered the water no closer to the hole -- (red staked hazards only) you'll find this is the easiest option in most circumstances. Simply go to where you believe your ball entered the water and drop a ball within two club lengths of the entrance point, as long as the ball doesn't end up closer to the hole.

CORY'S TIP: How to drop a ball

You get two club lengths to take relief so use the longest club in your bag: the driver. Grab your driver and two golf tees. Place the first golf tee at the edge of the water hazard where the ball entered, then measure two driver lengths away from the hole and away from the hazard and then place another tee. Drop your ball anywhere in between the two tees.

FAR: Some golf courses will have what's called a 'Drop Zone' near a hazard. So if you hit your ball into the water, have a look around to see if you see one. If there is one, simply take your new ball and drop it anywhere in the indicated area. Take your shot from here but remember to take your one stroke penalty!

Rule 13-4. Ball in Hazard

"Prohibited Actions Except as provided in the Rules, before making a stroke at a ball that is in a hazard (whether a bunker or a water hazard) or that, having been lifted from a hazard, may be dropped or placed in the hazard, the player must not:

☐ *Test the condition of the hazard or any similar hazard*

☐ *Touch the ground in the hazard or water in the water hazard with his hand or a club; or*

☐ *Touch or move a loose impediment lying in or touching the hazard."* *

CORY: A bunker is a hollow where the turf has been replaced with sand. Kids call it a sand pit, or some people refer to it as the beach, but the proper term is to refer to it as a bunker.

If your ball lies in a bunker the main thing to remember is to never touch the ground or ground your club in preparation for your shot. Your club must hover. Another important thing to remember in a bunker is to never remove any loose impediments that lie within the bunker. So if there are rocks, pebbles or twigs in the bunker you cannot move them until you are done with your shot.

FAR: Honestly, I think this rule is ridiculous. If there are some pebbles and twigs and leaves in the bunker, I think I should be able to remove them if it doesn't affect the position of my ball. It's already hard enough that you have to hover your club and can't touch the sand with your club before you hit the shot. However, I don't make the rules of golf and hopefully this one will change in the next revision of the rules!

Lost Ball & Out of Bounds Rules

Rule 27: Ball Lost or Out of Bounds

*"Ball Out of Bounds – If a ball is out of bounds, the player must play a ball, under penalty of one stroke, as nearly as possible at the spot from which the original ball was last played."**

CORY: First things first: every golfer loses golf balls. It happens to the best golfers on TV, so don't beat yourself up over it. Out of bounds areas are identified with white stakes. If your ball crosses into an out of bounds marked area, you cannot play your ball and you must return to where you initially hit your ball from and re-hit taking a one stroke penalty. That's right - whether you hit out of bounds on your tee shot or in the fairway, you must go back to the spot you initially hit the ball from and hit again! It's important to notice what colour the stakes are. White (out of bounds) means you must re-hit, red (hazard) means you can hit from where the ball entered the hazard!

FAR: Most often the out of bound or OB stakes are there to delineate golf course property from residential property or roads or sensitive areas that no one wants you in. So if the ball is outside the white staked area please don't go and get it. Yes it may be clearly visible and it may be your lucky ball, but it's out of bounds now and deserves to rest in peace. Besides, you could be charged with trespassing!

❑   Five Minute Rule

"If, after playing a shot, you think your ball may be lost outside a water hazard or out of bounds you should play a provisional ball. You must announce that it is a provisional ball and play it before you go forward to search for the original ball. If the original ball is lost (other than in a water hazard) or out of bounds, you must continue with the provisional ball, under penalty of one stroke. If the original ball is found in bounds within 5 minutes, you must continue play of the hole with it, and must stop playing the provisional ball."

FAR: Okay here is how this works: If you've hit your shot and you think (or know) that your ball is lost, you should hit another shot from the same position you took your first shot from. This is called hitting a 'provisional' and it gives you a playable ball in case you can't find the first one. Then you have five minutes to go bushwhacking through the woods or swamps in order to find your first ball. If you don't find it, you can play your provisional with a one stroke penalty. If you find your ball, and it is in bounds, you can play it without penalty and simply just pick up your provisional and put it back in your cart. If you know you don't have much of a chance to find your ball, you're better off declaring it lost, taking the penalty and continuing with your provisional. But what is most important is that you have five minutes to look for your ball before you give up and move on. Personally, I think one minute is long enough, but that's me.

CORY's TIP: How to count your score with penalty strokes

An easy way to help count out your score with penalty strokes is to replay each time the ball was moved saying the stroke number after. So let's say you hit it in the water and you re-hit it from the tee. Then your first tee shot that went into the water was one, the act of dropping the second ball on the tee is two, your re-hit is three. So now you are lying three on the fairway, you hit the next shot on the green, that's four, and then you putt five, and putt again six - to get it in the hole. I say in my head each shot and drop and say the stroke number after, it really helps count out your total score on the hole and to understand how the penalty has impacted it.

Knowing the rules summary

Don't let the rules of golf take away your joy of hitting a great shot or making a big putt. You'll find that lots of people play the game but don't actually know all the rules or apply them correctly. If you are playing in the Club Championships, yes it's important to follow the rules of golf, but if you're out having a fun game with your friends, don't get too hung up on them.

To recap the more common rule situations:

- Play your tee shot in between the tee markers.

- Do not touch the ground in a hazard, with your hand or golf club.

- Do not move loose impediments within a hazard.

- Lateral water hazards are marked with red stakes.

- If your ball goes into the water you have the option to play it or re-hit. If you re-hit you have the option to drop where you initially hit from, drop behind the water, or drop within two club lengths from where your ball entered, no closer to the hole, all under the penalty of one stroke.

- You only have 5 minutes to locate a lost ball.

- If your ball is lost or out of bounds, you must replay your shot from where you initially hit from, under the penalty of one stroke.

- Out of Bounds are marked with white stakes.

I encourage everyone to know how to find the rules of golf, especially if you want to play more golf. What if the person you are playing with, your boss or your potential client, is a stickler for the rules? Some golfers will buy a rule book and carry in it their golf bag so that they can reference a rule if necessary in a serious round. To find the official rules as of 2017, use the link below. There is talk of rule changes for 2019 that will be easier to understand and make sense to implement. This is a great step in the right direction so please make sure you stay on top of the new changes as they roll out.

*Reference:

http://golfcanada.ca/app/uploads/2015/03/2016-RULES-OF-GOLF-Final-single-pages.pdf

Joan's Story: *"I started playing golf for exercise and fresh air and to network with other women. My position in sales and marketing in a mostly male environment gave me the opportunity to do business on the golf course with corporate customers and I realized quickly that it is not necessary to excel at golf to be respected.*

I love the game and my interest is in mentoring women who want to learn the game. I volunteer with the GIRLS GOLF program and I help promote learning the rules of golf. I have been involved with golf though my business and sponsorship of golf events keeps me deeply involved with all aspects of the golf community. I get a lot of support for my business from the golf events I get involved with." Joan Davis

CHAPTER 7

YOUR GOLF PERSONALITY

Of all sports I have played in my life, golf is hands down the most frustrating and hardest game to play well. When you take a test, it's done in private and the mark is confidential, but on the golf course your performance is visible for everyone to see. This is especially frustrating, not least to mention intimidating when you are just learning the game. No matter what your skill level is, you will always hit a few (or a lot of) shots that you'll find embarrassing; it's the humbling nature of the game and you just need to accept and manage it. Which, of course, is easier said than done!

Yes, learning to swing a club is difficult, but learning to manage your emotions on the course is far more challenging. For the pros, being able to rebound from a bad shot is critical to winning a tournament. For recreational players, a bad shot or series of shots can ruin your mood for your entire afternoon if you let it.

Of course you will rarely be playing golf alone, so not only do you need to manage your own emotions, you'll need to manage your reactions to other people's emotions. How will you respond when someone in your foursome blows up in anger, or sulks, or cheats and sucks the energy out of your group? It certainly makes for an awkward networking opportunity and can ruin the next few hours and all the hard work you have put into creating this relationship building opportunity. This is especially difficult if that person is your boss or a client.

You can't control how others will emotionally react to their games, but you can control your own emotions! Remember the most important *Smashing The Grass Ceiling* concept: **it is not about your ability to swing a club that matters, it's about being the kind of person other people want to play golf with.** You want to be positive, helpful, attentive, understand the etiquette and rules of the game and generally be a fun person to be around. Do that, and no will care what your score is!

In this chapter I will outline some of the most common golf personalities you'll encounter on the golf course. You will at some point be playing with a group of golfers who have difficult personalities, so recognizing this and knowing they exist will help you deal with them appropriately. More importantly, if you recognize yourself as one of these personalities, then start finding ways to change it now!

The angry golfer

The angry golfer has been immortalized in many golf comedies and quite often resembles a child throwing a tantrum! They will smash their club on the ground after hitting a bad shot, yell expletives, kick the cart tire, break clubs or even throw clubs in the woods or water!

While you hope that angry golfer can recover their equilibrium after a few holes, often it will destroy their round and make it very uncomfortable for everyone playing with them. It's a surefire way to ruin a good time and it doesn't portray them in a positive light to their playing partners. Imagine if they get that angry about a golf shot, what does that say about how they will respond when a business situation doesn't go their way? Let alone manage a business emergency?

The excuses golfer

I could write an entire chapter on the amount of excuses I have heard from golfers who hit a bad shot. I hear it all the time when I outdrive people off the tee. "These aren't my clubs," "I can't play in the wind," or "this is my first round of the year" are just a few of the ways these golfers can't take responsibility for hitting a bad shot!

One of the things I am always reinforcing to my team at work is that we will all make mistakes, we are human. But when you make a mistake, take responsibility for it, own it and use it as an opportunity from which to learn. Making an excuse every time you hit a bad shot shows to your playing partners that you are not able to take responsibility for your actions. I guess that would be ok if you never made mistakes, but that's unlikely, so taking responsibility is a sign of maturity and professionalism.

The apologetic golfer

The trademark of this golfer is apologizing before every shot and telling everyone how bad they are before they even swing. Come on, would you ever stand in front of your board members or peers to make a presentation and apologize first that your presentation will be bad? How many times in your career or job have you 'faked' it? You do it because you want to show confidence.

If you are a beginner, your group will know you are new to the game before you play so there is no need to keep apologizing all through your round! You may not feel confident when you are playing golf, but for crying out loud, don't show it! Be confident to be better.

The silent sulky pouty golfer

You will feel this golfer's energy before they even say a word because the worse they play, the quieter they become. They internally obsess over their bad shots and can't let it go to move on and hit their next shot. In many ways this can feel more oppressive than the angry golfer's outbursts.

This was me one time on the Futures Tour, and it was so horrible I have banished this persona from my life! I was in Colorado playing an event and I just couldn't adjust for the altitude. The high altitude makes the ball fly further, and I already hit a long ball, so I was overshooting a 300 yard fairway out of bounds, which means I was slapped with a two stroke penalty every time. I was over hitting every green even after I thought I adjusted for it by hitting two clubs less than I thought I would need. It was extremely frustrating because I was hitting well but I couldn't be an angry golfer because people were watching, so I became silent sulky pouty golfer and it ate away at me the entire round.

I was a horrible person to play with until the 15th hole when I realized my score was so bad that I wasn't going to make any money anyway, so I just relaxed and enjoyed hitting my 9 iron 175 yards! I made a par and two birdies on the last three holes. If only I had been able to manage my emotions earlier.

This was a valuable lesson for me and one I have carried with me ever since: you can't play well when you are caught up in your emotions. The faster you can get yourself out of the mood, the better you will play and the more fun you, and everyone around you, will have. Don't doubt the impact your mood has on everyone you play with. Don't be the person who brings your group down.

The know-it-all golfer

You know this person. This golfer likes to tell you what to do in any situation, often unsolicited, and likes to show off their knowledge of the rules of golf. Or maybe it's more appropriate to say their 'alleged' knowledge! Whether they are right or wrong is beside the point, because being told what to do constantly is annoying. Maybe it's just that they like to hear themselves talk or that they are feeling insecure and therefore have to show off how smart they are or how well they know the game. What I do know is that once I have endured a round with them, I won't play another round of golf with them again.

The cheater

Nobody likes a cheater. Nobody respects a cheater. Nobody forgets a cheater. There are a million reasons for why someone might choose to cheat on the course. Cheating comes in many forms. Not counting your strokes properly is the most obvious. Saying you shot a five when you really took eight strokes to put the ball in the hole. Cheating is also dropping a ball when you lost your first one and saying you magically found it, or pretending to check and see if the ball is yours and miraculously giving yourself a better lie in the process.

Here is the main point. If you have decided as a group to keep score, then keep an honest score. If you are playing a casual round of golf but are still keeping score, keep an honest score. If you are not a strong golfer and will be easily embarrassed by your high score, don't keep score. And please, please, please don't brag about how well you played when you didn't keep an honest score. That will annoy everyone. So when it comes down to it, don't cheat. All you will do is build a reputation of being untrustworthy and no one wants to do business with someone they can't trust.

The oblivious golfer

For me, this is probably the most frustrating type of golfer to be around. They are never ready to hit when it's their turn because they are too busy talking or not paying attention. They want to go to the bathroom after you have already driven past it and are at the next tee. They leave their clubs behind on every hole, they never know where their own ball is let alone anyone else's and they don't think ahead and park their cart in the most inconvenient places!

Don't use being new to the game as an excuse for being oblivious. Be respectful of your playing partners and respectful of the game. If you are oblivious on the golf course what impression are you leaving about your ability to manage a project or do your job?

Too many practice swings golfer

This golfer usually takes five or seven practice swings and then still hits a terrible shot! While it may be an important process for them to follow, it is very frustrating to stand around and wait while they do it, and it slows down the game for everyone. I always encourage my students to take a good practice swing. This means you must hear the 'swish' as your club brushes against the grass on your practice swing. If you don't hear that sound, then take another. Fidgeting, swinging, double checking your aim, shifting your feet, more swings, checking again, more swings and then finally hitting the ball is painstaking for everyone. Take a good practice swing, address the ball and swing with confidence.

Your golf personality summary

What do all of the golf personalities described above have in common? You wouldn't want to play a round of golf with them, therefore you are not likely to want to do business with any of them! I think of golf a bit like the Hulk. You start out your round as this nice polite person and then, bam, something about playing the game triggers the emergence of these personalities! Whether you turn inward and become silent, apologetic or make excuses for your game, or you turn outward and become a know it all, an oblivious or angry golfer, in all cases your energy will affect your playing partners and will ruin a fun day out.

Pay attention to the personalities of others around you and golf becomes a very valuable HR tool. The anxiety that comes naturally when you are not at your most competent needs to be managed constantly on the golf course. Keep your emotions in check, stay positive and learn a few basic rules and etiquette. It will make you more confident, more enjoyable to play with and help you build strong connections with the people you are playing with.

Shannon's Story: "My mother remarried and my new step-father was a member at a course. Literally within a month of joining I met the man who would become my husband. The game brought our families together and it also created an experience my husband and I could share and enjoy.

I took to it quickly and I loved the exercise, the remarkable scenery and the great people I could meet. When my career started to excel I also quickly realized golf was a tremendous way to get clients out of the office and stuck with me for six hours – something a lunch meeting can never accomplish. As importantly, it was something I could do with my male clients without it ever crossing any lines.

It's a great mental test and one of the best business related undertakings you can do. The network and relationships you can foster on a course are unprecedented. Do it. Be okay with being okay as it has taken even the best of the best time and practice. Have fun when you play. Life is far too serious. Remember golf is a game not a war with a ball. Pick up the ball when you get frustrated and move on". Shannon Bowen-Smed

CHAPTER 8

PLAYING BY 'FAR'S RULES'

So far in this book I've given you a lot of information about the aspects of golf that are rarely taught outright. Most of the information concerning how to get yourself around the golf course, rules, etiquette and appropriate behaviour is learned by playing with other people. Depending on their comfort level, they may try and teach you or they may feel like it's not their place. But trust me, they will notice your behaviour and make judgements about it. Suffice it to say, it's hard to learn the nuances of the game without feeling intimidated or stupid and these feelings are some of the main reasons that prevent women from playing golf.

I haven't achieved success by being conventional all the time and golf is a hard game to play, so I have adapted and now play by my own set of rules – a set of rules that still enables me to be respectful, but also helps me to enjoy the game more and make it easier to play. In this section, I will introduce Far's Rules, which are strategies to help you manage your emotions, keep up in your group, and become the perfect playing partner for anyone on the golf course.

Far's Rules are designed for those who are playing recreationally and do not apply in a competitive round of golf. I certainly did not invent all these strategies, but have seen them used and have used them myself and they work wonders. Remember the intention is to become the golfer everyone enjoys playing with. Be sure to establish with your playing partners ahead of time whether you will be playing by the actual rules of golf or Far's Rules! You can't use Far's Rules if you are keeping score – they are purely designed to keep the game moving at a good pace and to keep it enjoyable for everyone.

Don't keep score

My days of keeping score when I golf for fun are long gone. It adds an element of anxiety that I don't need in my life. While you should know how to keep score because it's a good way to measure your progress, my advice to all beginners is to not do it for at least your first ten rounds. Learn the game, play it, and enjoy it first before you start adding a whole new dimension of competition and anxiety around it.

Also, please try and remember that you are only playing against yourself when you play golf. The point is to beat your own best score. This is difficult to remember when you are playing with other people as you'll want to compare yourself against them and their score. It's a natural reaction and if you are at all a competitive person, it will be irresistible, but trust me, you will not be doing yourself any favours. It's hard enough to remember all the etiquette and manage your emotions on the golf course as it is, so don't add any more challenges to the mix.

Focus on being a fun player

What is the most important part of playing golf? Your score? Your swing? What you're wearing? NO! The most important thing is that you have several hours to spend with people in a non-distracting environment. Golf gives you precious amounts of time to get to know someone and build a deeper relationship. You have an opportunity to establish a connection with a potential client and have them get to know you better as well. People will do business with people they know and like.

Your goal is to be the person that everyone wants to play with because you don't get hung up on the small stuff and you keep the game moving with a positive attitude. **It is very hard to network or do business on the course with someone who is frustrated with their game, counting every shot, following every rule and playing slowly.**

Solidifying your relationships is the most important reason for being on the golf course. That's the big picture. You will have more bad rounds than good ones, you will hit more bad shots than good ones. No one will tell you this but the game is actually about the quality of your misses, and if you realize that going in, you can frame your expectations better. Focus on being a fun player to be with and you will find that your game will take care of itself.

Managing stress is critical

Stress is as prevalent on the golf course as it is in your professional life, especially when playing with people you want to do business with or your boss and coworkers. Imagine your stress level when you've just hit your ball into the water three times in one hole! Or when you take four swings and totally miss the ball all four times! **Your ability to handle stress on the golf course is paramount to your success in using golf as an effective relationship building tool.**

So how do you handle stress out there? Here are some easy tips to help you stay calm out on the course and have some fun:

Don't hit your first tee shot

First tee jitters are common with almost every golfer. It always feels like everyone is watching you and it's hard not to feel pressured to hit a good shot. As easy as it may be for me to say it, don't start your round with jitters and stress. Simply skip your first shot and decide to start your game out on the fairway. Tell your playing partners you are not quite ready to hit yet and drop a ball anywhere in the fairway or over by a playing partner's ball. You're not keeping score, so who cares? There's no reason to start your round with anxiety.

Forget about bad shots

Remember that you will hit more bad shots than good shots in your early golfing years. So, if you have hit your ball two fairways over, leave it. Someone else will surely appreciate a free ball! Don't fuss about running over to find it and then trying to put it back in play again. Who needs that stress? Just drop another ball in your fairway a reasonable distance away or next to one of your playing partners and hit from there.

Let lost balls lie

If your ball goes into the thick rough or the woods, spend about a minute looking for it and not a minute more. It's frustrating to keep looking for balls, it holds up your playing partners, it takes you off your rhythm, and you'll probably just get dirty, bedraggled and covered in bug bites. A ball isn't worth it. They're easy to come by and they're sold in dozens for a reason! By the rules of golf we spoke about earlier, you have five minutes to look for a ball, but seriously, five minutes? If you are playing for fun, have a cursory look and then move on.

Tee it up

If you are struggling to make contact with the ball on the fairway, use a tee. By the actual rules of golf you can only tee your ball up on the first shot of every hole. However, teeing up on the fairway is a common strategy used by many novice golfers when they are first starting out. I know lots of women who are afraid of hitting the ground and getting injured. As you gain confidence, only use a tee for longer shots and hit off the grass once you get closer to the hole.

Use a foot wedge or a hand wedge

If you don't like where your ball is sitting (on a root, in a divot, in really thick weeds, on the side of a hill, in the bunker, etc.) kick it out into the open, or even throw it onto the fairway, and hit it from there. It's hard enough to hit a ball when it's on the flat fairway, don't stress yourself out and kill your confidence trying to make shots even the pros have trouble with!

Keep the game moving

Missing the ball, or 'whiffing' it is a common occurrence for new golfers and a big source of stress for the person swinging away. Don't get caught up with making contact all the time. If you take two swings and miss the ball both times, pick it up and move on. Throw it next to your playing partner's ball down the fairway. Seriously, who cares? It's way more stressful to keep hacking at it while people are waiting on you. Keep it fun. Keeping up is so important that the entire next chapter is devoted to it.

Water? What water?

If you need to make a shot over water and you know you can't clear it, don't hit the shot. There's no need to lose a ball and get discouraged. Go to the other side, drop your ball and start from there. If you are the type of person who does not get frustrated easily then sure, go ahead and hit it, and if it goes into the water then oh well. And when you make it over the water, its celebration time!

Scramble it!

If you know you are the least experienced player and are concerned about holding people up, play a scramble using your playing partner's balls. By this I mean, hit your shot and if it is far behind the rest of the group's balls, pick it up and drop it near theirs and hit your next shot from there and continue this way until you putt on the green. You'll play faster, you'll hit less balls (so you won't be as tired) and you'll have more fun.

If all this seems unconventional - well it is, and I love it! Why struggle out there and be frustrated when you can play the game and have fun.

If you are not keeping score, you don't need to swing the club every single time.

Far's Rules in action

Here's a story about my friend Michele who used Far's Rules to keep her round stress free and manage her emotions. We set up a round of golf with myself, my mum and my friend Rosanne at the gorgeous Dundas Valley Golf & Curling Club. Dundas is a difficult course and Michele disclosed that she was not a very good golfer, but she really wanted to be part of our foursome and come out and spend the afternoon with us. Of course me, being super encouraging as I usually am, reassured her that it would be totally okay because we were just playing for fun and it didn't really matter how good she was.

On the first tee, the three of us had great tee shots. Michele stepped up to the ball and hit it three feet. She laughed at herself, something any confident person needs to be able to do, and brushed it off as no big deal.

Michele then says, "I'm going to play a scramble. Rosanne, I like where your ball went and I'm going to hit my second shot from your position." She picked up her ball, went to Rosanne's ball and hit her second shot from there.

Michele continued to hit every shot by playing a scramble with whoever's ball she decided she liked better and we had a GREAT time! And when she hit a decent shot, we all cheered! We had a wonderful afternoon and she was able to enjoy the day of networking and relationship building by using a very smart strategy to manage a potentially anxious and difficult situation.

Playing by Far's Rules summary

If you disclose to your playing partners that you are playing by Far's Rules before you start they will appreciate your ability to remain positive and your self confidence in adapting the rules to make them work for you.

No one thinks you are a bad person because you play bad golf! But no one likes playing golf with (or doing business with for that matter) a petulant, moody, negative person. If you can make yourself feel comfortable with how you are playing then the others around you will feel comfortable too! They won't feel sorry for you if you don't feel sorry for yourself!

Please remember that you cannot use Far's Rules and still count your score. However, if you have a good hole, celebrate it, cheer, high five, have a shot of Fireball, do whatever you need to enjoy that feeling, because it is a good feeling and we need more good feelings in our lives no matter where they come from.

Michelle H's story: I've been playing golf for over 10 years and when I started I was terrible. I used the same techniques as Far's Rules. I teed up the ball down the fairway, I regularly picked up my ball to keep up pace of play and I never kept score. What was most important to me was participating. I hated being left behind while my partner and friends were out playing. I had a great time on the course and didn't care how well I played. As long as I kept up and didn't get frustrated, we all had a fabulous time out. It's ironic that now that my game has improved I find it much more difficult to manage my emotions on the course. Far's Rules are a good reminder to not take the game so seriously and focus more on being a fun playing partner than a great golfer!" Michelle Harris

CHAPTER 9

KEEPING UP

All golf courses set a target timeline in which it is reasonable to finish a round of golf. This is known as the 'pace of play' and when you are out on the course, you need to be respectful of the guidelines. In my opinion this is probably the most important thing that all golfers need to know. If you can keep up with your group and keep up with the group ahead of you, then you will remove a lot of the anxiety and stress. Often courses will have marshals to help keep the pace of play on schedule. Play too fast and you will be pushing the group ahead of you, play too slow and you will be annoying everyone behind you! The previous chapter on Far's Rules had some strategies to help you manage your frustrations, but in reality, all of Far's Rules are designed to help you keep up with the pace of play.

No matter what caliber of golfer you are, being able to keep pace with your group and the group in front of you is critical to successful interactions on the golf course. Those are big words I know, but trust me, they are true! In this chapter I'll give you some surefire strategies to manage your pace and therefore your stress level so you can have a great time out there and focus on your relationship building.

Play ready golf

'Ready golf' is a commonly used way of keeping up the pace of play in a casual round of golf for networking, in charity events or with your family or friends. Ready golf means hit when you are ready, not necessarily when it's your turn. You would not use ready golf if you were playing a competitive round of golf where your score counts.

By the rules of golf, the ball that is farthest away from the hole must play first. It's called being 'away.' When someone is away, it's their turn to hit next. You may hear, "am I still away?" or "you're away." Whoever is away is the one to hit the next shot. If you are not away, but your ball is nearby and you notice that your playing partner is not quite organized yet to hit their shot, then use the rules of ready golf and hit if you are ready.

I am not suggesting that you rush your shot, but if you are ready and can hit safely, go ahead. Ready golf can also apply on the tee shot. Technically, if you are playing from the same set of tees, then whoever shot the lowest score on the last hole gets the honour to go first. However, if they're not organized, it's okay to remind them politely that it's their turn to go and if they say go ahead, then whoever is ready should go. The appropriate thing to do with your playing partners is to establish right from the first hole that you will play ready golf and that your intention is not to usurp anyone's rightful turn to play, but instead to keep the pace moving.

Ready golf can also apply on the green when putting. If the person who is farthest away from the flag is still raking their bunker for example or hasn't approached the green yet, it's okay for the others to start putting. Alternatively, if you are paying attention and thinking ahead, you can offer to rake the bunker while your playing partner proceeds to their ball to hit their next shot.

Plan ahead

Keeping up takes some forethought and planning. When out on the course always be planning your next shot. **While waiting for your playing partners to hit, think ahead to your next shot.** Can you safely go to your ball without distracting your playing partners? How far away are you? Which club are you going to hit? Where are you going to aim?

That way when it's your turn to hit, you'll have your club in hand and be ready to take the shot.

> Far's Tip: waiting an abnormally long time for the group ahead of you to get out of range so you can hit is unfortunately a common occurrence on busy golf courses or during charity events. If your ball lies ahead of your playing partners and you all have to wait, then go to it, do all your decision making on what shot you are going to hit and where, and then go back to wait with the rest of your group so you can continue to network and spend time together. When it's your turn to hit, you're ready to play.

Don't keep score

The one thing that slows down the pace of play tremendously is when every golfer in your group is counting every single swing. This is of course common practice on the professional golf tour, and I will be the first to admit that many pro golfers have a hard time keeping up the pace of play. When your pay cheque is determined by whether or not you make the next 4 foot putt, you will take as much time as you can to line it up and breathe so you can stay calm!

I grew up golfing with Mum who got annoyed very easily when she was stuck with slow players, so my regular pace of play is inherently quick. However, I learned my *hakuna matata* (Swahili for 'no problem') from my dad who is the quintessential example of patience. As I said earlier, I rarely keep score during a casual round of golf.

This game has so many nuances and is challenging in and of itself that when you add the element of counting every stroke it can become quite disheartening and take a long time to play. If you are playing a non-competitive round of golf, but want to keep score to measure your progress, use the other strategies suggested to help you keep up the pace of play.

Quit after double par

Every hole has a 'par' which is the reasonable number of strokes a professional (or someone just as good) can finish the hole in. For example, a par 4 hole means that a good golfer should be able to hit four strokes to put the ball in the hole. Most golf courses will have a few par 3s and par 5s and a bunch of par 4s.

If you are new to the game, a good rule of thumb is to max out your strokes at double par. This is a reasonable number of strokes to take for a beginner and it will help you from getting too frustrated while keeping up the pace. So, if it's a par 4 and you've already hit 8 shots, pick up your ball and move on to the next hole. There is no shame in picking up the ball! It will be a relief for you and it will be appreciated by your playing partners (and the group behind you.) I run a bunch of charity golf events and I always have the double par rule clearly stated in the rules for everyone to follow.

Take only 4 shots to get to 100 yards

Another strategy for keeping up the pace of play is what I call '4 to a 100.' This means that if you have hit four shots and you are still not inside the 100 yard marker, pick up your ball and take it there. This will still give you the opportunity to practice different shots and keep you moving at a nice pace. Obviously you won't be keeping score while using this strategy but you can still measure your success by trying to get to 100 in under four shots. It's unconventional, but then again so are you!

What to do when you fall behind

You will know you have fallen behind the pace of play when the group ahead of you is long gone and there is a group behind you waiting on every stroke. If you just can't catch up and you are holding up the group behind you, it is time to let them 'play through.' I have played many rounds where the group in front of me should have let us play through but didn't. Sometimes this is because people don't know how to do it so they just speed up instead and rush themselves. Letting the group behind you play through is a win-win for everyone. You will appreciate not being pushed and feeling rushed and the group behind you will appreciate not being held up.

How to wave a group through

In my experience the safest and easiest way to wave a group through is on a par 3. Have your group tee off. Then go to the green, mark your balls and move off to the side and indicate to the group behind you to tee off and play the hole. When they are finished, go back to your mark and finish playing the hole. When you need to wave a group through and there isn't a par 3 handy, then tee off at the next hole and wait at the tee decks to indicate to the group behind you that you are letting them play through.

How to play through

If your group is playing well (way to go Smashers!) you might be waved on to play through the group in front. If they are letting you play through, make an effort to finish your shot and get going! It's common to feel rushed when playing through because you have been given the opportunity to go and you want to move along. You also now have four new people watching you play which can add a whole new element of anxiety! Just stay focused, hit your shot and don't forget to thank the group for letting you play through.

Every experienced golfer has encountered a group of golfers who will just not budge and let the group behind them play through. Usually this group of golfers wrestles with ego issues and tries to justify all the reasons why they are not at fault. Maybe angry golfer resides in this group and they just can't see past their emotions to be considerate of others around them! In this situation you can ask the marshal on the course to intervene on your behalf. Many times a group of women golfers will be stuck behind a group of men who are not keeping pace and they are not waved through because the perception is that the women will be slower players. In actual fact, I think women play faster than most men, but the guys are just not used to that yet!

Keeping up summary

Make no mistake, the more times you swing, the slower your pace of play will be, so naturally a beginner will take more time to play than a more experienced golfer. However, if you play ready golf, think ahead and know your scoring limitations, keeping up with your group and the group in front of you will become so much more manageable and you and your playing partners will enjoy your round of golf more. It is much easier to facilitate a business conversation if everyone is having a good time and in a great mood. Use Far's Rules and these strategies to maintain the pace of play and you will enjoy the experience in a positive manner and it will make you a better golfer.

Maggie's story: *"The one thing no one ever really considers is what your life will be like when you are older. What happens is that your friends pass away. Sure, you may have children but let's face it, you can't control when they visit. What you can control, is how many times a week you golf. Golf provides a venue where you interact with all age groups and ensures you will have friends for the rest of your life."* *Maggie Loefler.*

CHAPTER 10

MASTERING CHARITY TOURNAMENTS

I think the biggest opportunity to use golf as a networking tool is to play in tournaments. For some of you, you may have picked up this book because you play in one tournament a year and you want to be more confident on the course. For others, you might be ready to take a group with you to a tournament and want to know how to leverage the event to its fullest.

No matter where you live, there are plenty of charity and corporate events happening at golf courses throughout the season. Golf tournaments provide the perfect venue to spend several hours with people you want to connect with. I cannot tell you how much it pains me to go to a golf tournament and see the women working the registration table or volunteering while the men are out there playing and having fun. Let's smash that grass ceiling and get out there! Be confident and use the opportunity to get to know people and have people get to know you.

Given my golfing background you would think that I would jump at the chance to attend any event I was invited to, but that wasn't always the case. When I retired from tour golf and got a 'real' job as I called it, I hardly played golf at all. While I was building my business and busy growing my family, my golf game deteriorated and I felt embarrassed to play with anyone who knew me. ("She was on the tour? No wonder she didn't make millions!") I lost out on so many opportunities to network and create meaningful, strategic relationships through golf because I was embarrassed about my game – yes, me the professional golfer. How much sense does that make? When I finally realized that people would not judge my abilities as an entrepreneur based on my golf skills, I started to play more and to enter into more charity events. I was only able to handle about five rounds a summer as I was building my business and starting my family, but every time I played, I made a new connection. And as I mentioned earlier, the more you play, the better you get, the more confident you feel out on the course, and the easier it is to focus on relationship building! Tournaments are the ideal environment to practise everything I have talked about so far in the book!

Besides being a fun day out of the office, entering a golf event also positions you and your business as a community supporter and allows so many networking and marketing opportunities. You can sponsor a hole, donate a prize or auction item, and meet lots of new people. If it's a charity event, then you are doing something good just by being there, and as my dad always said - the more you give, the more you get. *Make entering golf events a part of your marketing and promotions budget.* It's that important.

All golf events will have either a lunch or a dinner or both included, so treat it like any other networking event, bring business cards and wear your branded corporate clothing. There will be a lot of time spent waiting on the golf course either at your hole or in between holes so there will be time to network with your own group as well as meet the group in front or behind you as you wait for play to move along.

Go it alone or bring your own group?

The first decision to make is whether or not to enter the event alone or bring three others to make your own foursome. There are pros and cons to each choice but the most important thing to remember is that you are not going to be evaluated on the caliber of your golf game but on how you manage your interactions on the golf course. Just like in your business or corporate job, you must appear confident at all times and that only comes with knowing how to behave in different situations. Remember you can be the worst technical golfer in the group but also be the most fun person to go to a tournament with.

The advantage of entering an event alone is that it provides an opportunity to gain some confidence while simultaneously using golf events to build your brand and your network. You will meet more people when you can circulate the room and it's cheaper to enter as a single instead of as a foursome. Entering an event alone is much harder socially especially if you are shy. I always make it a point to get to know the organizer and request that they put me in a group that is fun or strategic to my needs.

In general, I prefer entering my own foursome because then I choose who I want to spend time with and I have much more control over how the day will go. If you are playing with clients, employees or potential clients, remember you will be evaluated by them based on their experience throughout the entire day. While this may seem stressful, it is an incredible opportunity to make a favourable impression. Therefore it is critical that you know how to manage the experience from the moment you enter the golf course until you send them on their way home. I will take you through the ins and outs of a tournament so you will be uber prepared for hosting a group at a charity golf event.

You are the CEO of your foursome - act like one

If you are bringing a group, treat it like you are the CEO of this team. You own this interaction and the success of the day lies squarely on your shoulders. **This is a huge opportunity for you to create a favourable experience, demonstrate your attention to detail and show your ability to manage people.** Right from the start when you send out the invite to join you to play, start asking questions. Find out if anyone is familiar with the course you are playing. Ask if they would rather be a driver or a passenger in the cart. And most importantly ladies, let them know your skill level so that you set the expectations from the very beginning. It's ok to tell them that you are entering a non-competitive team and the intention is to get away from the office and have some fun while supporting a good cause. Decide on a meeting place and time at the event and be sure they have your contact information.

> Far's Tip - Usually the registration area is a good meeting point and suggest to your group to arrive one hour before the start time to have enough time to have a meal and warm up properly.

Do you need a change of clothes for dinner?

While not everyone's first question, it's important to know. Find out from the event organizers ahead of time what the culture of the event is after the golf portion is over. Do most people bring a change of clothes or are golf clothes appropriate to stay in? You don't want to be the only one wearing shorts and a golf shirt when everyone else is wearing dress clothes!

For the majority of the events I've played in, I stay in my golf clothes and just freshen up a little after the game. I change my shoes, maybe change my shirt at the most if it's too sweaty. There have been some events where the dinner is a dress up affair, in which case I bring a full change of clothes! Either way take your freshen up bag with you as there is probably a locker room you can leave it in so that your deodorant doesn't melt in the car!

Arrive at the course early

Arrive at the course at least one and a half hours ahead of the start time. Why so early? You want to give yourself enough time to settle, get the lay of the land and prepare for the day. As you drive up to the course you will be greeted by a course representative who will take your golf bag out of your trunk for you. When they ask for your name tell them whether or not you will be the driver or the passenger so that they know where to place your bag in the cart.

> Far's Tip – check with the greeter that the names of all your group members appear on their list. Mistakes can happen and you want to ensure your group does not start their day in confusion because their name was missed in error.

The registration table is your central hub

All events will have a registration table which is the check in point for the event. In most charity events in North America, each group will start on a different hole. The organizers will have a list with your name and starting hole number and the names of your playing partners as well. If for any reason you have not paid the registration fee yet, you can do it here. I know it doesn't need to be said, but please be nice to the volunteers at the registration desk. Ask their names, introduce yourself, find out how their day is going so far. Remember these are the people you will go to for help to solve any issues during the day!

The volunteers will ask if you want to buy mulligans (a mulligan is a free hit or a 'do over'), raffle or draw tickets or to enter any of the special events on the course that are taking place that day - the appropriate answer here is YES! This is a charity event and they depend on you for support so be open to the suggestions. Usually this means anywhere from $20-$50 so please carry some cash. If you have been invited as a guest of someone's to this event and you haven't paid the entry fee, then you most definitely should buy any additional items – it's the right thing to do.

Eat before you play

Golf tournaments take a notoriously long time to play so be prepared for a very long and tiring day. I can't say this more emphatically. Make sure you eat before your group arrives. You want to be on the top of your game and ready to point them in the right direction when they arrive. It may end up being a hot day and there will be alcohol around so be sure to give yourself the best chance of success with your group. Getting drunk after an hour is probably not the best way to make a favourable impression!

> Far's Tip – Bring snacks for your group to leave in the cart. A bag of nuts or bars and some easy-to-eat candies that won't melt in the sun are a good way to give someone a little boost during a long day outside, and it shows that you are a considerate person and thinking of the group.

Warm up before you play

Once you have eaten, take some time to warm up before your group arrives. It is important to warm up because not only is it a good stretch for your body, but it also helps gets the nerves and rust out and leaves you feeling a lot more confident. Your clubs will have been placed on your cart and each cart will be numbered and parked sequentially by starting hole number. Find your cart and grab a couple of clubs to take with you to the driving range.

> **Far's basic warmup routine**
>
> Warm up balls are usually provided on the driving range at most events. Grab your wedge, 7 iron and driver. Put a few tees in your pocket and don't forget your glove. Start the warm up by hitting a few short chip shots with your wedge, then progress to half swings and then full swings. Switch to your 7 iron to make a few full swings and then hit a few drives with your driver. End with a few more short chip shots. Once you're warmed up (10–15 minutes max), hit a few practise putts on the putting green.

Be at your cart 15 mins before start time

Once your group arrives and everyone is fed and warmed up, be at your cart and ready to go 15 minutes before the official start time. If you have entered alone, this will be where you will most likely meet your playing partners. Reinforce to your group your skill level to set their expectations. Remember to carry yourself with confidence.

Take this time to get yourself ready to play. I usually like to pull out three golf balls and keep them in my cart, because let's be realistic, I will lose at least two and depending on the day I may lose eight! Keeping a few in the cart saves time rifling through your bag to find balls when you need them. Keep some tees in your pocket as well as a marker and a divot repair tool.

The event organizer will call people to their carts, make any pertinent announcements and will refer you to a rules sheet that is probably on your cart already. Once the introductions are over they will lead you out to your starting hole.

Shotgun start

Most tournaments will have a 'shotgun start' meaning that there will be a group or two starting on every hole instead of groups teeing off from the first hole in succession like tournaments on TV. A full golf course has 18 holes and a full shotgun means that there are 36 foursomes playing in the event or 144 golfers. In a full shotgun, every hole will have an A and B group. Once everyone gets to their starting hole, you will usually hear an air horn signalling play to begin. I really like the concept of shotgun starts because everyone in the event starts and finishes together which is efficient and good for networking.

If you ever get a chance to play in one of my women-only Smashing Nines tournaments, which I hope you do, it's a 9 hole shotgun. That means there is only one group on every hole. The intention is to not have a group breathing down your neck from the start so you can relax and learn to play with others and build your confidence. We play 9 holes, have lunch and are done! Start at 10 am and done by 2pm. The point is to have some fun and to learn how to use golf as a networking tool.

Getting to your starting hole

Depending on the event, you may not be starting on the first hole. You may be assigned '5A' for example, which may be right in the middle of the course. The course marshals know the lay of the course and as long as you follow them and their instructions you will be fine! The marshals will lead you out in order. Pay attention to the holes as you drive by them and when you see yours, peel off from the group and park there. If it's a full event and you are on 5A, chances are there is also a 5B group. The A group goes first and then the B group, but if your group would rather go second, let the other group go first. Sometimes it's hard to hit the first shot with people watching so give yourself the best chance of success. Someone in your group should be responsible for keeping your team score, so be sure to designate it.

How to play a scramble

Usually tournaments play a format called a 'scramble.' A scramble is when all four people tee off, then the team decides who has the best shot, the other three pick up their balls and drop them near the one they want to use. Everyone then hits their second shot from that position, pick the next best ball, and so on and so forth until the ball is holed out. Often this scramble format is referred to as best ball, which is technically incorrect. Best ball is when everyone plays their own ball till the end of the hole and then you choose the best score out of the group.

What I love about scrambles is that it enables beginner golfers to play with more experienced golfers and allows everyone to feel a part of the team. I mentioned the scramble format briefly when we talked about Far's Rules as a strategy you can use if you are the weakest golfer in your group. Remember the story of Michele and how she was able to use the scramble as a strategy to keep up with more experienced golfers in her group?

A quick word about scramble events. The rule of thumb is that the best ball is marked with a tee so that the position is saved. Everyone else then drops their ball within a club length (3 feet) of the marked position as long as it is not closer to the hole. If the best shot is in a bunker, everyone must play from the bunker. If you bought mulligans at registration, be sure to use them. A mulligan is a free hit, so don't leave them unused!

Special contest holes

During the round there may be some special contests like longest drive, closest to the pin, chip into a bucket etc. Some events require a minimal fee for these when you get to the hole, others will have made you pay for them at registration. Never a bad idea to have some extra cash in your pocket - remember it is a charity event! Be sure to engage with the volunteers on these holes as well, they will have been outside for 6 hours doing the same thing for every group and they will appreciate being acknowledged. One last thing, to qualify for closest to the pin your tee shot must be on the green, and to qualify for the longest drive your ball must land on the fairway. Usually these holes will have a metal stake with a piece of paper attached to it so that you can write your name down and mark your position.

Mastering charity tournaments summary

Let me reiterate that tournaments are an excellent way to practice playing golf in a relatively stress free environment and they provide an excellent venue to show off your people skills. The price range for entering into a tournament varies depending on where you live, but the average price in my area is between $175- $275 per person to enter, unless it is a specialty event. Talk to your accountant about the best way to claim the expense as a deduction. I highly encourage you to **budget for at least four golf tournaments per season** at the minimum. Choose ones that cater to your target market or support a cause you believe in.

Amy's Story: I started playing golf because it gave me an opportunity to bond with my girlfriends and not be pressured to "impress" as you sometimes have to do when you golf with the men. Personally it has built a larger network of girlfriends who I can golf with when I retire in the future. Another benefit is the exercise, I do not use a cart and I find my core is stronger for it. Go and take lessons so you can learn your own "bad habits." It can be very frustrating trying to hit the ball and it only goes 10 ft. I would hate for someone to quit the sport before they even get a chance to try it out, take lessons and golf in a ladies league for the support." Amy Kasianiuk

CHAPTER 11

HOW TO DO BUSINESS ON THE GOLF COURSE

Everything that we have talked about so far in the book will help you do business on the golf course. Whether it's during a tournament or you've invited a client out for a round, playing golf is a tremendous opportunity to get to know someone better and build a relationship outside the office environment. Men have been using golf for years and there's no reason why women can't do the same thing. It takes confidence, knowledge and common sense and those are three traits that women I know pride themselves on!

Once you get your potential client or boss on the golf course, now what? Timing, as they say, is everything. Whatever you do, don't overdo it. This means, do not ruin this precious time you have just facilitated into one long drawn out business discussion. In fact, I recommend playing it cool and not seeming overly eager to talk shop. You are there to build a relationship first, so focus on that and the business will come. That being said, in this chapter I will outline some concrete advice for doing business on the course.

Dress appropriately

This may seem pretty obvious to most people, but please be sure to dress appropriately on the golf course. Obviously tank tops and crop tops are a big no-no, but there are some fundamental things to pay attention to when dressing for the game. First, you will be bending over, so watch for low cut shorts or pants and wear a belt if you need to. You will also be swinging and rotating your torso, so if your shirt is too short, it will rise up and expose your belly on your swing.

Golf fashion is always evolving and acceptable standards change constantly, but you will never go wrong if you follow this basic dress code:

- Collared shirt

- Bermuda shorts

- Capris or pants

- Skorts

- Socks

Use common sense and foresight when planning for your round. If rain is in the forecast, obviously don't wear a white shirt please! Take rain gear with you and a change of clothes for after if you think you might get soaked.

Lastly, it's always a good idea to find out beforehand if the golf course has a dress code. For example, men might not be allowed to wear cargo shorts or even any shorts at all! Some courses require that men wear long pants or that they have to tuck their shirts in at all times. Imagine inviting that key potential client out for a round and he isn't allowed on the course because of what he is wearing.

Be on time

Just like any professional appointment, you should always be on time to make a favourable impression. Being on time is respectful and a normal expectation when you attend a business meeting, so no reason to think that being late for a round of golf is acceptable.

Ideally you want to be as relaxed and comfortable as possible. Arriving early means you can warm up, grab a drink for the course, chat with your playing partners and get prepared for your round. Arriving late will leave you feeling panicked, disorganized and your energy will affect those you are playing with.

As I discussed in the previous chapter about being the CEO of your foursome, you want to arrive earlier than your guests so that you can facilitate their experience from the moment they arrive. Think of it like having a guest in your home. You want to be ready to receive them when they arrive and make sure they are well catered to.

Stay sober

Drinking alcohol on the golf course is not something I grew up with in Mombasa. We had small huts on our course where you could get a drink of water or some fresh squeezed lime juice. Having drink carts circulate the course was a concept I learned after I came to Canada. While many golfers appreciate the ability to enjoy a cold beverage on the course, you should be mindful of the effect of alcohol on your game, your mood, and your playing partners. Think of it like a business lunch. Does it feel appropriate to have that glass of wine with your meal or not? You obviously know your own limits, but on hot days alcohol can hit you a lot faster than in normal situations. Always have bottles of water in your cart and some snacks to help out your playing partners or yourself. Remember alcohol heightens your emotions and loosens your inhibitions. Two things that are not particularly helpful on the golf course, and definitely not when you are trying to woo a new client or make a favourable impression with your boss.

Know the outcome you want to achieve

Whenever I go to any networking event I have a strategy in mind for how to break the ice and make a lasting connection with new people. I usually like to talk about travel. I am always looking for new travel destinations, so I ask people about their favourite vacations. It makes for easy conversation and people tend to remember me because it's not a typical networking conversation and it reminds them of happy memories. Similarly on the golf course, you should always know what your desired outcome is for the day. Are you trying to convince them to buy your product or service? Are you looking for their capital, expertise or connections? Are you trying to deepen your relationship with your boss so that you might get a promotion in the future? No matter the reason, know the outcome you want to achieve so that when the right opportunity arises you will be able to take advantage of it!

Never talk business before the 3rd hole

My rule of thumb is to never start talking business before the 3rd hole and always stop after the 14th. You want to give your playing partners a chance to warm up and get into the game and, frankly, after 14 holes most people are just plain tired. If you are out for 9 holes, then wait until the 3rd to talk shop and stop talking business after the 7th hole. Of course, if your guests start talking business then follow their lead, but know when to stop.

Golf is an emotional game so pick the right opportunity to start your discussion. If the potential client, vendor or employer you are playing with has become angry golfer on the golf course, it's probably not the right time! On the other hand if they have just hit a great shot and are all smiles, go right ahead and start to engage and take advantage of the positive endorphins flying around. Pay attention to their mood and pick the right opportunity. It might never arise if they are having a miserable day and that's okay, focus on building a connection instead.

Keep up and respect the game

I can't stress enough how important it is to keep up the pace of play and follow good golf etiquette. If your client is a much better golfer than you are, they will appreciate it when you pick up your ball and keep moving. **No one wants to watch someone self-destruct on the course - it brings everyone down.** Stay positive, pay attention, use Far's Rules and be respectful to the game. Trust me, do this and you will leave a much more favourable impression than if you had shot the best score of your life. I can't say this enough times, you don't have to be a good golfer to do business on the golf course. You do need to manage your emotions, follow good etiquette and be confident. Your goal should be for your guest to say, "that was the most fun I've had playing golf in a long time." Do that, and you can guarantee that they will play with you again, talk about you favourably and most likely be amenable to whatever business goal you had with them!

Have your brand visible

We discussed briefly in the tournament section about wearing your branded clothing to the course. You are out there representing yourself, so have your brand visible. If you are committed to using golf to build your business, then get a few collared shirts embroidered with your logo. If you have company branded golf balls, give your playing partners a sleeve of balls before the round starts. After the round, be sure they leave with your business cards. Golf bags have several pockets in them, so make sure your bag is always stocked with cards.

Be nice to people

It seems trivial to say "be nice to people," but you would be amazed at how often we miss opportunities to do just that. If you are a nice person, are likeable and can carry a conversation on the golf course, people will want to do business with you.

Want to know the easiest way to make this impression? Be nice to the staff on the golf course! When you see the grounds crew working diligently, smile and wave at them as you drive by. This shows that you acknowledge and appreciate all their hard work to keep the course in great shape. Talk to the beverage cart servers with respect and tip well. I cannot tell you the amount of times I have heard crass, rude and generally inappropriate comments directed towards the beverage cart servers. There are many opportunities to engage and treat golf course staff with respect and gratitude.

It also never hurts to give compliments to your playing partners on well hit shots. People like receiving compliments when they do something well, so be the bearer of nice words when it is justified. If you put that positive energy out there with intent, it will find its way back to you tenfold.

If you invite, you pay

If you have invited people to play with you then you should pay for their round. Discussions around money can be uncomfortable, so be very clear when you are inviting your group out. Tell them they are there as your guests and be sure to get to the course early so that you can take care of their green fees before they arrive. I have been caught in numerous situations where I was asked to join a foursome and when I got to the pro shop to check in they asked me how I was paying for my round. My assumption was that I was invited to play therefore my round would be taken care of.

Ask your group beforehand if they want to walk or ride and remember to pay for the carts as well if you are hosting them. Getting a round of golf is like buying lunch for a client meeting. It's the cost of doing business. Ask your accountant about writing off golf expenses before you head out so you know what receipts you need to keep for them.

Practise makes perfect

You may need to play in a few tournaments, or with friends and family first to build some confidence on the golf course before you venture out to play business building rounds. Ladies leagues are a great way to meet other women who golf at a similar level as you. Once you build up some confidence, make a tee time with a friend and let the course match you up with others on the tee. It's a great way to network, make new connections and practise playing golf with strangers.

Doing business on the golf course summary

While the golf course is not a boardroom, it a good idea to think of it that way. All the same advice for making a favourable impression holds true. Be on time, dress appropriately, and be strategic about your outcomes. Moreover, manage your alcohol intake, market your brand, play the game with the strategies I've outlined in the book and be a likeable nice person that others want to spend time with. Remember if you invite others to play, you should always foot the bill. Treat it like you would a business meeting and be sure send an email reminder the day before the round and then a thank you email after.

When the sun is shining and you are enjoying a relaxing day on the golf course, it can be easy to lose focus and treat it like a vacation from the office. Trust me, men who are out on the course with clients are very strategic about what they are doing and so should you!

BE A SMASHING GOLFER!

I want to thank you for making it to the end of this book. Your time is valuable and I hope I have given you the confidence, knowledge and strategies you need to get out on the course and *Smash The Grass Ceiling* with me!

I never realized until I became a business owner the skills that the game of golf has been teaching me my whole life. What started as a selfish way to spend more time with my mum has become a tool that I credit with the success and opportunities that I am so grateful to have experienced. Golf has given me the ability to stay calm under stress and to manage difficult situations and people. My decision making, patience, integrity, problem solving and conversation skills all came through the game of golf. Skills that I use on a daily basis in my role as a business owner, wife, mentor, mother, athlete and volunteer.

My first exposure to public speaking came through golf. When I won a tournament I would always have to make a speech. Now I get hired to deliver keynote speeches on topics such as volunteer motivation, how to be better, using golf to enhance your relationships, emotional intelligence, and driving to success.

When I was on the mini tours grinding it out as a professional golfer I had more bad rounds than good rounds (when you play more, you will find that out as well). Dealing with those bad rounds was a constant challenge and it required a lot of energy to talk myself out of feeling like a total fraud. The guilt and embarrassment of posting a bad score were like anchors weighing me down. Then when I started my entrepreneurial career, I can remember waking up anxious in the middle of the night because I was so afraid others would realize that I really didn't know what I was doing! Being insecure and feeling fear are normal reactions to new experiences. It's how we deal with them that matters most and it is a trait that most women I know are built to handle!

Please remember that playing bad golf doesn't make you a bad person. How you carry yourself on the course makes all the difference. Being positive and using the knowledge and strategies in this book will make you a golf partner that everyone will want to play with. Ladies, stop apologizing for your perceived lack of ability. You don't step into a client pitch and say "oh this presentation may not be very good." If you lack a skill in your work environment you take a course to make up the deficiency. If you want to play better, take lessons and get reasonable equipment. Carry yourself with confidence and a sense of humour and it will take you far.

If you become angry golfer or silent sulky pouty golfer or any of the other golf personas we talked about before, you will draw negative attention toward yourself. Your playing partners will appreciate it far more if you radiate positive energy while you are playing, and I can guarantee it will make your round a lot more enjoyable as a result. You will be known as the person who is great to play with and, personally, I like to do business with people I enjoy being around!

Throughout this book I have talked about all the different skills golf has taught me. I was fortunate that I started young. I had my mum as my golf mentor and my dad as my business mentor, as well as a handful of other strong women leaders I am so fortunate to know. I believe in order to keep *smashing the grass ceiling* we need to encourage girls to get involved in the game early. The 'Smashing Girls' program was designed to give teenage girls a unique opportunity to learn golf while interacting with professional women mentors on the golf course. I want the girls in our program to see that even if their mentors are not hitting perfect shots, it doesn't reflect on the success they have had in their lives. The way they carry themselves is what defines their character. The mentors in the program are all volunteers and I hope you decide to be a mentor one day to help shape our girls into *smashing women*. You can find out more about the program on my website: www.farsamji.com Proceeds from the sale of this book will go towards enabling girls without means to participate in the Smashing Girls program.

Finally, I want to encourage you to use the opportunities the game provides to be better. Use it as a stage to showcase your ability to try new things, to go with the flow, take some risks and thrive in uncomfortable situations. Show off the skills that make you the amazing, incredible and accomplished woman that you are! Watch as the preconceived notions from your peers fall by the wayside as they watch you own your game and handle pressure with grace and positivity!

Be a Smashing Golfer.

Thanks for reading,

Far

EQUIPMENT SUMMARY

Below is a chart of the most common golf clubs, a ballpark of how far they should go and when you would use them.

Remember:

☐ Irons differ by loft (the angle of the clubface) and length

☐ Irons are numbered - the higher the number the shorter the club

☐ The shorter irons will go higher (8, 9) & the longer irons will go further (6, 7)

☐ The sand wedge (SW) has the most loft and the shortest distance, followed by the pitching wedge (PW)

☐ Hybrids should go further than irons and can be used from the rough. They are a good option to advance the ball down the fairway

☐ Fairway woods go further than hybrids but can be harder to hit and should be only used on the fairway or with a tee for the tee shot if your driver is not behaving!

- A driver is used at the start of most holes (except some par 3s) and you use a tee to raise the ball off the ground. A ball hit with your driver should travel the farthest.

Club Name	How Far will it go?	When do I use it
Sand Wedge (SW)	10-50 yards Depends if you are hitting a short chip shot or a longer shot over an obstruction	In the sand, or for short shots onto the green where you need to get good height
Pitching Wedge (PW)	10-80 yards Depends if you are hitting a short pitch shot or a full shot	Hitting a shot onto the green, or if you need to hit over an obstruction in your way
Shorter irons (8, 9)	80-110 yards	Hitting a shot onto the green
Longer irons (6, 7)	110 - 140 yards	Advancing the ball on the fairway or hitting from a difficult lie or the rough. You can also use these clubs for tee shots on shorter par 3s
Hybrids (4, 5, 6)	140 - 160 yards	As your second shot and maybe third shot from the fairway or rough. You can also hit them as your first shot on a par 3. Generally easier to hit clubs and can be hit as 'rescue' clubs

Fairway Woods (3, 5, 7)	150 - 175 yards	As your second shot and maybe third shot when on the fairway. Also as your first shot if you have difficulty using a driver. You can also hit them as your first shot on a par 3
Driver	140 - 200 yards	For your first shot, using a tee
Putter	Inches - several feet Depends on how far away you are from the flag	On the green or from just off the green if the grass is cut short enough

COMMON GOLF TERMS

A

apron: also known as the fringe; the short grass that separates the putting green from rough or fairway

away: the player farthest away from the hole

B

back nine: the last 9 holes (10-18) of an 18 hole golf course

bag drop: the area where you drop off your bag when you arrive at the course to prevent you from having to carry your bag from the parking lot

ball mark: also known as a pitch mark or divot; the depression that a ball makes when it strikes the ground

ball marker: a small, flat object used to mark your ball's position on the green while other players putt and/or you clean your ball

best ball: an event format where everyone plays their own shots until the ball is holed out and then the best score is taken as the group score. Often mistakenly used to describe a scramble format

birdie: a score of one stroke less than par for a hole

bogey: a score of one stroke over par for a hole

break: the curve of a putt due to the slope of the terrain

bunker: also known as a sand trap or the beach; a depression in the ground filled with sand

C

caddy: someone who carries your bag of clubs and/or assists you with advice and the details of play

casual water: temporary puddles of water on the course which are not supposed to be there, like after a rainstorm. There is no penalty for you to move your ball out of casual water

chip: a short approach shot with a low trajectory usually hit from close to the green

chip in: when you hit a chip shot into the cup

choke: to grip lower on the club than normal (to 'choke down' on the club); or to collapse under pressure (she 'choked')

chunk: hitting the ground before the ball, usually results in the ball not going as far as you would like

cup: generically refers to the hole but also includes the sleeve inside the hole that holds the flagstick in place

D

divot: a piece of ground that is ripped up by your club after hitting your ball

dogleg: a hole where the fairway has a bend in it like a dog's rear leg. A dogleg left means the fairway bends left.

double bogey: a score of two strokes over par for a hole

double par: multiplying the par of a hole by two, and the maximum amount of shots you should hit on a hole as per Far's Rules

drop: you take a drop if you have hit your ball into an area that you can't play your next shot from (out of bounds, pond, etc.) This is usually assessed a penalty stroke

duff: a bad shot

E

eagle: a score of 2 strokes under par for a hole

executive course: a golf course with shorter holes, mostly par 3s and short par 4s

F

fade: a gently curving shot from left to right (for a right handed golfer)

fairway: the closely mown area between the tee and green

fairway bunker: a sand trap or deep grass hazard beside the fairway

fore: to be yelled out in warning if you hit a shot towards another person on the course

front nine: the first 9 holes (1-9) of an 18 hole golf course

G

gimme: a putt that is short enough in length to be certain to be holed with the next stroke

green: also known as the putting green, putting surface, or dance floor; the most closely mown area on the course designed for putting your ball into the hole

H

hazard: any sand trap, lake, pond, bunker, etc. that may cause problems on the golf course

heavy: a shot where you hit the ground before the ball, usually results in the ball not going as far as you would like; as known as 'chunking' the ball

holing out: used to describe the act of finishing the hole by putting the ball into the cup

honour: the privilege of playing first from the tee

hook: a shot that travels from right to left (for a right handed golfer)

hybrids: a type of club that is a cross between an iron and a wood. Usually used on the fairway or to rescue you out of tough areas

I

Irons: a type of club that has varying loft and lengths. Shorter irons have more loft and less length than longer irons

L

lay up: a shot played to a particular location to allow for an easier next shot or to keep the ball from going too far

loose impediment: any natural object that is not fixed or growing (e.g., rocks, twigs, leaves, etc.)

M

mulligan: taking a second attempt at a shot when you are not happy with the result of the first attempt; also known as a "do over"

P

par: abbreviation for 'professional average result'. This is the standard score for a hole or an entire course that a professional is expected to make

peeking: looking up to see the result of a shot before impact

playing through: the process of allowing faster players behind your group to move ahead of you

pitch shot: a relatively short, lofted shot designed to land softly and not roll much

provisional ball: a second shot played in a situation where you believe that your original ball may be out of bounds or lost

R

reading the green: determining which way the putt will curve based on the slope of the green

rough: longer grass adjacent to the fairways, greens and perhaps tees.

round: a complete circuit of 9 or 18 holes

S

score: the number of strokes taken on a hole or course

scramble: a tournament format in which all players in a group hit a shot from the tee, and each subsequent location, always playing from the position of the best or preferred ball until the ball is holed

short game: the part of the game that consists of short range shots like chipping, pitching and putting

shotgun start: a golf tournament format in which all groups of players tee off simultaneously from different holes

T

tap in: also known as a gimme; a very short put that is certain to be made

tee: a small peg you put in the ground to sit the ball on top of; to raise the ball off the ground

tee deck: the area marked by tee markers where you would hit your tee shot from

tee shot: the first shot on a hole

tee time: the time assigned for a group to begin play on their first hole

tending the flag: holding and then removing the flagstick after a player has made a stroke. This allows players to see the hole when lining up long putts

W

wedge: a type of club, usually the shortest in a set, with the most loft

waving through: the act of sending the group behind you ahead of you because you have fallen behind the pace of play

WANT MORE FAR?

KEYNOTE SPEAKER

A naturally charismatic and energizing speaker, Far is continuing to expand her availability as a speaker to professional associations, corporate and not-for-profit audiences. Far's life experiences as an elite athlete, entrepreneur and philanthropist inform a variety of speaking topics and insights about what it takes to be a successful entrepreneur, volunteer, businesswoman and leader. Her unconventional approach to business and life is a refreshing perspective that has audiences both large and small "paying attention" and challenged to rethink their own approach to business and life. Hire Far to deliver your next keynote speech.

GOLF TOURNAMENT PERSONALITY

You will want Far to make appearances at your golf tournament and provide an interaction experience with your group that will leave them inspired and motivated. She can provide *Pre-Tournament Clinics* to participants and host a *Beat the Long Drive* hole at events. The tournament package also includes remarks at the Tournament Lunch/Dinner. Have Far at your next golf event, and your guests will be amazed, inspired and motivated to return to your event.

SMASHING NINES

Smashing Nines, are women's only nine-hole golf tournaments. The event is a perfect setting for women to experience tournament play in a fun and relaxed environment. You will experience first-hand the power of the game to help you build networks, relationships and your personal brand. Contact Far if you want to host a Smashing Nines event in your area.

LESSONS AND BOOTCAMPS

Contact Far to set up golf lessons or boot camps for your company or for you and a friend to learn all the Smashing techniques in a small group environment. Or check her website for the upcoming boot camps, lesson clinics and golf retreat that you can join.

BE A MENTOR FOR SMASHING GIRLS

Smashing girls is a program designed to teach girls 13-16 life skills through golf and mentorship.

FOR MORE INFORMATION

Farsamji.com   **longdriver@farsamji.com**   **289-259-8132**

Mentors are professional women, not professional golfers! Contact Far to become a mentor.

**Proceeds from the sale of this book will go
to the Smashing Girls program**

The *Smashing Girls* program is designed to give teenage girls a unique opportunity to learn golf while interacting with professional women mentors on the golf course. Our girls are inundated with images of perfection in how they should look, eat or behave. These perceived notions foster them to create unrealistic expectations of themselves. Help me smash this attitude. I want the girls in our program to see that professional women who hit imperfect golf shots, can still be successful. The way they carry themselves is what defines their character. The mentors in the program are all volunteers and I hope you decide to be a mentor one day to help shape our girls into Smashing Women.

The program:

☐ Five weeks of instruction

☐ Each girl gets paired with a volunteer mentor

☐ Two rounds of golf at Dundas Valley Executive Course - each foursome consists of two girls and two mentors

☐ Instructors circulate during the rounds

☐ Mentors commit to entering one charity tournament with their mentee. This teaches them the nuances around entering an event, talking with other adults, silent auctions, raffles, sharing a meal with strangers and other great skills

Monies raised are used for:

☐ Transportation for the girls

☐ Equipment for the girls

- ❑ Instructor fees

- ❑ Green fees (mentors pay their own way)

Girls are identified for the program by various local youth focused charities that have established mandates for providing opportunities for kids.

All mentors will go through a screening process.

If you would like to make a contribution to *Smashing Girls*, please visit www.farsamji.com

ABOUT THE AUTHOR

Fareen "Far" Samji is a 5-time ILDC Canadian Women's Long Drive Champion (2012-2016). With a personal best Long Drive of 334 yards, at 5'5" tall, she is considered small for the sport, proving that bigger isn't always better... better is better. And, at only 42 years old, she has achieved success as an entrepreneur, an internationally acclaimed athlete, and a community leader.

Born and raised in Mombasa, Kenya, she immigrated to Canada in 1988. At 16 she started at McMaster University, in Hamilton, Ontario and earned two degrees (Psychology and Kinesiology). In 1999, Far earned her tour card and competed on several pro golf mini tours around the world.

After leaving pro golf, she joined forces with her brothers to start a successful family business. Over the past 15 years the company has expanded to include three orthotic and orthopedic shoe clinics and an orthotic manufacturing facility.

Far discovered the sport of Long Drive in 1994 but didn't really start competing until 2012. Undeterred by her size disadvantage, in 2012 she won the first of five consecutive ILDC Canadian Long Drive competitions, and in 2015 she won her first International ILDC Championship.

With a drive to help others, Far leads by example as an active rotarian and supporter of several community events. In 2014 she joined Jason Davies to co-found the *Board of United International Long Drive (BUILD)*, a not for profit association dedicated to furthering the sport of Long Drive throughout the world.

As an active rotarian, Far has been involved in many initiatives, and is passionate about Service Above Self. With boundless energy and a charismatic personality, Far Samji is a successful entrepreneur, golf instructor, keynote speaker, celebrity host, mother, mentor, volunteer and author. Fareen currently lives in Burlington with her partner and their two teenage kids.

Printed in Great Britain
by Amazon

18827565R00073